Perhaps the best way to learn leadership is to surround oneself with authentic leaders — and that is exactly what David Irvine and Jim Reger have done for the readers of this book. Its pages are packed with real-world examples of the challenges — and rewards — of being an Authentic Leader.

— **Norman R. Augustine**, *Retired Chairman & CEO, Lockheed Martin Corporation*

Join the authors — and all the wonderful people they talk with — on their travels through life toward authenticity. Take a journey toward your true self by accompanying others on their journeys. Their experiences will hearten and inform you.

— **Geoff Bellman**, *Consultant and Author of* **Your Signature Path** *and* **Getting Things Done When You Are Not in Charge**

The true essence of leadership is service and moral courage. Both service and moral courage are enhanced by authenticity. David Irvine and Jim Reger have greatly facilitated our understanding of how to empower and synergize our collective productivity with **The Authentic Leader**.

—**Dr. Len Marrella**, *Founder and President, Center for Leadership and Ethics, and Author of* **In Search of Ethics**

This book brings to life the notion of "authentic leadership." It adds the magic sauce and thus the DNA.

—**Sam Georges**, *CEO/President, Anthony Robbins Holdings*

For years we have heard that leaders must be authentic; finally someone shows us what that means. David Irvine and Jim Reger are the real thing, authentic leaders helping other leaders become more real. Of all the soul's desires, being true to self is the greatest. David and Jim show us how to reach that desire. This book is an excellent treatment of an important topic and leaders who want more influence and more joy in leading must read this book.

— **John Izzo**, *Author of* **Awakening Corporate Soul** *and* **Second Innocence**

Too often, the journey in life is a thorny experience involving erosion of our souls. Myriad forces conspire to have us give up our authentic selves to serve the dictates of hierarchical power-based structures.

At last, this book has arrived, addressing this dilemma by offering holarchical solutions to reinforce the development of the human in the midst of an ever-depersonalizing world.

This important writing is at once informative and inspiring. We are pleased to have had the opportunity to participate in its creation. We recommend it highly.

— *Bennet Wong*, *M.D. F.R.C.P. (c) and Jock McKeen*, *M.D.*, *F.R.C.P. (c)*, *Authors of* **The New Manual for Life** *and Founders of The Haven Institute*

I believe the time is right for this book as so many people I meet are thirsting to fill a void of significance and meaning in their lives. The words of the authors and others describing their quest for purpose and authenticity are gifts to consider as we each find our way.

—*Judy Walton*, *Vice President of Human Resources (Canadian Region), Conoco Phillips*

I have read many leadership books over the years; most taught how to lead like others, either directly or through their ideas and ideals. Finally I read a book that teaches me to lead like ME! For every leader struggling to find their way this book will be a revelation. The fact that my authentic self will become the core of how I lead will revolutionize not just my leadership but its impact for the future.

—*Lawrence Barns*, *CEO, The Canadian Association of Family Enterprise (CAFÉ)*

What the world needs now is a book about being authentic. Years ago, leaders discovered the words "empowerment" and "teams," but it became only rhetoric. There was a disconnect between the action and the words. People became confused with the lack of authenticity. Finally, a book that describes how important it is for the words and the actions to be one, and reflect the true meaning of respect and integrity.

This book will be especially important to women leaders — now and in the future. Caught in hierarchies which profess inclusion and empowerment, but where autocrats still rule, women are caught between two realities. Being true to who you are and what you believe about people, and being authentic above all else, is the key to success for women, both as individuals and as leaders.

Respect, kindness and integrity are signs of a truly authentic leader. This book has helped me understand that being "authentic" at work and at home is not a hat you put on when it's convenient — it's a way of being.

In doing management coaching, I see managers who believe they have to act a certain way to be leaders, pretending to be strong and have all the answers. It isn't real and the people they work with know it. Being "authentic" means being true to yourself and showing respect for others — that's what a true leader is. This book can lead managers and aspiring leaders down a path that validates being true to yourself.

    *— **Beverly Suek**, Former CEO of the Women's Enterprise Centre, and Director, TLS Enterprises*

The Authentic Leader

It's About PRESENCE, Not Position

The Authentic Leader

It's About PRESENCE, Not Position

By

David Irvine and Jim Reger

PRESS

A Division of the Diogenes Consortium

SANFORD • FLORIDA

Published by DC Press
2445 River Tree Circle
Sanford, FL 32771
http://www.focusonethics.com

Book set in Adobe Caslon
Cover Design and Composition by Jonathan Pennell

Library of Congress Catalog Number: 2006923981
        Irvine, David and Reger, Jim
The Authentic Leader
        ISBN: 1-932021-19-1
        ISBN: 978-1-932021-19-6

First DC Press Edition
10   9   8   7   6   5   4   3   2
Printed and bound in the U.S.A. Printed on acid-free paper

This book is dedicated to authentic leaders
who are committed to leading with presence.

Table of Contents

Prologue

This, above all: Unto thine own self be true.
— William Shakespeare

WHAT IS AN AUTHENTIC JOURNEY?

Reflect on a few questions:

- How do I articulate the meaning and purpose of my life?
- Who am I — beyond my positions and my possessions and my achievements?
- What matters most to me in life — beyond economic and materialistic success?
- What is the difference between making a living and making a life?
- How do I define success?
- What principles do I stand for that I will not compromise?
- What are my deepest unfulfilled dreams, passions, gifts?
- What kind of contribution am I making to the world — beyond self-interest?

If any of these questions resonate or if you struggle to find answers to them, then you have already started on what we refer to as an *authentic journey*.

An authentic journey is a path to finding your voice, to discovering your highest aspirations and purpose, to living an honest life, and to bringing your passions and gifts to the world in the form of service of others. It is a process that we also describe as *evolution of the soul*. An authentic journey is unique. For some, growth of the soul is a sudden *revolution*, a dramatic, life-altering upheaval, which causes dramatic transformation. Yet, for most people, growth of the soul is a gradual *evolution* into a new, slowly developing awareness.

Regardless of the path, an authentic journey ultimately leads to a deep, fundamental, and sustaining shift in self-perception and perception of your environment. This profound, life-changing evolution allows openness to realizing immeasurable potential and achieving the destiny you are meant to have. An authentic journey calls for self-alignment with a new reality through establishing new habits. Yet, it can also be a path to renewal in the workplace — an environment where the human spirit can become overworked, undervalued, and unfulfilled.

WHAT IS AUTHENTIC LEADERSHIP?

While an *authentic journey* begins with breaking away, at least in part, from the expectations of the world, but also remembering that one's true identity is found by retrieving and developing the soul, *authentic leadership* includes inspiring, guiding, and supporting other people to do the same. If you are engaged in uncovering and expressing your authentic self, and leading others on the journey, you know that this is both a challenging and a liberating process. It is a path to meaning, contentment, and deep satisfaction. It is the work to which we, as authors and leadership architects, are devoting our lives.

Len Marrella has written a book entitled *In Search of Ethics: Conversations with Men and Women of Character*, which is mandatory reading for every cadet at West Point. He expresses his thoughts about authentic leadership:

> I've always been convinced that in the end, our character is our destiny. People are irresistibly attracted to leaders of character because they can be trusted. It's hard to trust someone who is not authentic.

> People all over the world tell me they believe in honesty, respect (both of self and of others), responsibility, love, fairness, and freedom. These seem to be the "big six," no matter where I am in the world. However, when I take a hard look at what's going on, I find that there's a "disconnect" between what they say they believe and what they do, and authenticity is the bridge. I love that word "authenticity." I think it's the crux of everything. Authenticity and trust is what it's all about. If a person is authentic and trustworthy, they've got a leg up on everybody else, and that's in terms of personal happiness, as well as their success as a leader.

> Authenticity doesn't motivate so much as it *inspires* people. The difference between motivation and inspiration is a big jump. Motivation tends to be manipulation of personalities. Inspiration is a connection of souls. In my view, authenticity is about moral courage and servant leadership.

> I do believe that when someone trusts me and believes in me, and knows that I have a sense of fairness in terms of conversation and recognition, that I get so much more commitment, so much more empowerment, and so much more synergy. People can really commit them-

selves to what I'm doing, in terms of ideas, energy and productivity. When there are truly shared values, where the organization and the individuals in the organization are in sync, there is synergy. And the magic word is trust.

CHARACTERISTICS OF AUTHENTIC LIVING

Despite the diverse paths taken on an authentic journey, people that we encounter have similar characteristics or qualities. Living an authentic life requires:

- A dedication to seeking, discerning, and moving toward learning the truth about oneself; to accurately perceiving one's internal thoughts and external environmental events; and to discovering one's higher purpose in this life

- Knowing that authenticity is not about how much money one makes or about how much control one has, but is about the ultimate purpose of life, which is retrieving, transforming, and growing the soul. (Grace, prosperity, and inner peace naturally flow into this place.)

- Realizing that life is not about *proving* oneself or *measuring* oneself by the standards of others, but more about expressing oneself

- Making a shift from *conforming* to society's demands to having the courage to listen to and respond to the quiet call of the soul, finding that as one goes beyond economic and material success as a definition of self, a sustaining inner contentment emerges

- Learning that an authentic life is less about *self-interest* and more about *service*

- Having a willingness to grow rather than to maintain a pretense of perfection

In our collective 60 plus years of leadership development, counseling, consulting, and teaching, we find that many leaders have a strong commitment and a sense of urgency to "rediscover their souls" so that they have more positive presence in their leadership roles. We have also learned that certain *authentic moments* occur when one is connected to one's "true" self, to one's "own truth." When authentic moments are brought to the service of others, we identify this as *authentic leading*.

AUTHENTIC ACTIONS AND AUTHENTIC LEADERSHIP

We are passionate about learning more about authentic moments and the importance of their role in the work of leadership. To learn more about authentic moments, we embarked on a project to find and interview leaders who manifest *authentic actions*. Our goal was to use experiences of authentic leadership in story form to paint vivid mental pictures of what authentic moments might be like and then to learn how to bring more authentic moments to your work. We interviewed 37 people with a variety of leadership roles, e.g., in business, community development, the public sector, healthcare, education, the arts and physical disciplines, and in family roles. We will relate their stories to illustrate the power of authentic action. The stories are not to put any person on a pedestal of perfection, but rather they are to bring authentic actions to light. The stories simply relate experiences and authentic views, along with the contributions, the setbacks, and the lessons learned. These stories, along with our own perspectives, are to inspire you to persevere on your authentic journey.

THE CHALLENGE OF AUTHENTICITY IN LEADERSHIP

We believe certain actions or characteristics are authentic and thus are more powerful for leveraging one's impact. We also believe these authentic qualities are vital for effective leadership in the future. Although authenticity may be described differently, living honestly and authentically is inspirational. It is intricately connected to *leadership*. Living authentically can significantly impact a leader's influence. If one's purpose in life is to grow and to develop the soul, then as a leader, one's purpose in leadership is to help others grow and develop their souls.

Yet, leading is not a position. Leading is a decision. By our definition, when a decision is made to contribute to the betterment of the world (or to one's environment), one is a leader. The world desperately needs strong-hearted, authentic leaders. Authentic leading inspires, supports, and guides others to discover and express their uniqueness. Regardless of the leadership role, authentic leadership impacts others through the strength of an authentic presence. Whether one is a CEO, an administrative assistant, a parent, an artist, an elementary school principal, a community volunteer, a front-line nurse, a manager in a government agency, or even a person who is unemployed but has a vision, opportunities are available for authentic leadership.

Simply put, being an authentic leader is synonymous with being oneself. It is that simple, but it is also that difficult.

When deciding to lead, be true to self. Being true to self is being in a most powerful place. The power in leadership is not in being *right*, but in being *real*.

All the people we interviewed spoke about the perils of authenticity. Sometimes, especially at the beginning, authenticity is lonely. Being true to oneself, learning more about self (Who am I, really?), and finding and expressing a voice in the midst of the pressures of culture to conform are not easy. Living an authentic life is not immune to uncertainty, rejection, or fear, but at the end of the day, there will be self-respect from living in accord with certain values. Sam Georges, the CEO of Anthony Robbins Holdings, meets the challenge of leading authentically:

> The corporate model tends to use people like the pieces on a game board and becomes callous to the fact that each human being in the company is a person who has a soul and a history. The clothes they wear are really just a mask for their own fears and phobias, which probably are universal in the human realm, and each one of these people comes more than likely with the best intentions. What a leader really needs to do is to get out of the mindset of "the customer comes first," "the product comes first," "the plan comes first," or "the bottom line comes first," which is just another set of fears and phobias of the leader. They need to settle in to the fact that a leader's job is just to be available to the people. For me to arrive in a state where I can declare that I'm being authentic is a state where I'm not only operating out of my center, but I also feel the spiritual "grounded-ness" that goes with that, versus just the psychological notion of "centeredness." People deserve to be honored for who they are, regardless of my judgments about who they are or how they live. The importance of honoring people in the grace of who they are is the exercise of continually pulling away from those hidden needs to control, to use power, and to use force.

Though we trust you will find this book both inspirational and practical, it is not a how-to book. It is a book about having a more authentic life, from a more fulfilling perspective, and having a greater, more positive impact on others. If it were a how-to book, we would tell you how to do this, but then the book itself would not be authentic. We will simply relate lessons we have learned from our experiences and the experiences of others.

Carefully assess what you read and weigh it against the dictates of your own authentic voice, your own conscience. What happens when you are authentic? How do you feel when you are not? What are the consequences? Do you have the courage to do something about it?

It is not a book about getting ahead of others. It is a book about inspiring others. Our goal is to provide guidance and the permission to listen to your soul and to be more of who you are in your work of leading. In the process of leading, we encourage you to guide others to be true to themselves and to take the risk of leading authentically.

The practical lessons are to provide knowledge and guideposts that will support an authentic journey as well as a commitment to serve and influence others. They are to *inspire* (by painting a mental picture of authentic moments in leading), to *illuminate* (by shining a light on the actions of leaders), and to *instruct* (by suggesting practical strategies to put into immediate use to find your own voice while inspiring, supporting, and guiding others to discover and express their uniqueness). As leadership architects, we are committed to building foundations *within* people so they will have the strength of identity, integrity, and presence that supports a sustainable, life-giving culture — whether in societies, organizations, communities, or in families. First and foremost, our commitment is to support people to live in accord with their highest values, gifts, and purposes — their *authentic* selves.

BENEFITS VS. RISKS

Making a decision to embark on this very personal — authentic — journey will make a significant difference in every area of your life. Relationships will be more real. Work will be more fulfilling. Life will be more meaningful. You will be more connected to people you care about. Rather than maintaining a pretense of certainty, you will experience inner assurance in the midst of uncertainty. You may even sleep better at night.

Although taking on this lifelong quest — fueled by curiosity, courage, and a passion to grow — is a worthy goal, risks can accompany embarking wholeheartedly on an authentic journey. Yet, you will be reminded that the benefits of authenticity — not as a destination, but more as a method of travel — far outweigh the risks and disadvantages. To have a sustaining presence as an authentic leader, you must embark on an inner path of personal growth. This inner work precedes the work of developing others. Every action is a manifestation of who you are. By knowing yourself and bringing that self to your environment more courageously, your impact will be amplified on the people you serve.

OUR ROLE

Because we are lifelong learners and teachers, we will go on the journey with you. We are fellow travelers, offering, perhaps, more questions than answers. From our observations and experience, enduring leadership is much more about the identity and integrity — the inner presence — of a person than it is about techniques, quick-fixes, or superficial personality changes. *Character* development is more important than *charisma*.

Our commitment, therefore, is to provide support and encouragement to stay on your own unique path; to challenge you to go deeper into and farther along your authentic journey each moment of the day; and to inspire and challenge you to be more authentic more often. Above all, stay focused on the search. It is worth every risk taken.

SOME FINAL THOUGHTS

Ray Nelson once said, "It's easy to make a buck, but it's *important* to make a difference." This book is for people who are committed to going beyond "making a buck" to actually "making a difference." But what about the deeper needs of making connections, personal growth, making a contribution, and finding meaning? We live in challenging, demanding times, putting most of our effort into career pursuits, strategic plans, personal achievements, and acquisition of possessions while neglecting the things in life that really matter. Maybe it is time to step back from the rat race and find a better path.

May our words and stories awaken your thoughts and inspire you, while providing support and navigation for your authentic journey. From the strength of new awareness and new actions, may you develop renewed leadership perspectives that come from within.

* * * *

Acknowledgments

THIS BOOK IS THE RESULT of assistance from an amazing group of authentic people who participated in our learning and growth, stimulated our thinking, and supported us in innumerable ways. They also held us accountable to get this book written. Since taking on this project, we are amazed at the number of people who crossed our paths, how deeply they touched us, and how they enriched our lives, spirits, and thoughts about *authentic leadership*. They have our deepest respect, admiration, and appreciation.

DAVID

Anyone who writes and has a family knows that it is an author's intimate relationships that bear the greatest burden of sacrifice.

To Val, my life partner: Thank you for patiently supporting and encouraging my passion and dedication to this work. You are a gift. I would not be here today without your authentic presence. Thank you for your attention to detail in our family and in our business, for skillfully and endlessly editing early versions, and above all for your compassionate heart and unfailing love.

To Hayley and Chandra, my daughters who are still at home: Thank you for remaining supportive of your father's dream. Especially during the final months of writing, you remained supportive and were patient with my absences, even when you had little understanding of the magnitude of my deep commitment to this work. Hayley, you inspire me by your passion for the adventure of life. Chandra, you inspire me by your compassionate heart.

To Mellissa and Ramsay, who are following your own authentic path: Mellissa, you inspire me by your unique and special, creative presence. Ramsay, you inspire me by the calmness and ease with which you walk through life.

To Jim Reger: Thank you for joining this project with such trust and respect for the work. Your perspective, wisdom, and friendship continue to be a source of support and inspiration.

To Kate Harling, my sister: Thank you for unending inspiration and support of this work and for hours of conversation and passionate debate. Your affirmation, wisdom, love, and amazing authentic presence helped to make this book possible.

To Laurie Peck: Thank you for your unconditional support and encouragement. Your patience, gift of writing, and human perspective truly helped us get to the heart of what this book is meant to be about. Thank you for handling a myriad of business details to free up time for writing.

To George Masselam: Thank you for your life-giving friendship and insights into some of the early thinking behind this book.

To Barry Thorson: Thank you for the wisdom and inspiration that emerges from your authentic presence. You were particularly insightful in helping me craft my story.

To Sheila Tipping: Thank you for your professional work in transcribing all the hours and hours of interviews.

To Janet Alford: Your usual magic at structuring the early daft of this book was invaluable.

To Wendy Fuchs: Thank you for being a source of inspiration to everyone who comes into your salon. Your authentic spirit had an impact on this book.

To Warren Harbeck, David Stuart, Dale Kelly, Jim DeMesa, and Don Campbell: Thank you for reading the manuscript and providing invaluable feedback. The book is better because of your time, energy, perspective, and wisdom.

To Katharine Weinmann: Your perspective and affirmation, as we neared the end of this journey, was vital and precious.

JIM

To David Irvine: Thank you for pouring your heart and soul into this project and for allowing me to be part of the journey. Your vulnerability and courage have been inspirational during the many months that we have worked together.

To Joan, my wife and best friend for almost 40 years: Thank you for providing the love, strength, and support that were necessary for me to have the courage to explore my authentic self. Thank you for assisting me to be who I am. I cannot think of a greater gift.

To Natasha, my warm-hearted daughter, who changed my life forever on the day she was born: Thank you for the love I feel from you everyday.

To Brayden, my son, who is perhaps one of the most authentic people I know: Thank you for our conversations about life and its mysteries and magic. You are a wise old soul. I am thankful for your presence in my life.

To my sister, Loretta Baker: Thank you for being an anchor throughout my life. If I were to look in a dictionary under the word "service," Lorie's picture could be found.

To the team at my office: Deepest appreciation for your support — especially Vanessa Labossiere and Casey Norberg for assisting me with numerous versions of the manuscript and Zelda Dean for staying focused on the writing project discussed so many months ago.

To Brad Potentier, Starr McMichael, Joan and Gary Gagnon, Ryan Pettersen, and Walter Nicholson: Thank you for the time-consuming project of reading the manuscripts. I greatly appreciate your time and insights.

About the Authors

DAVID IRVINE

David Irvine, known as *The Leader's Navigator*, is an internationally sought-after speaker, author, and mentor. His work has contributed to building accountable, vital, and engaged organizations across North America. He is president and CEO of an international speaking and consulting firm that specializes in leadership development. Over the past two decades, David has delivered over 1500 workshops and presentations to thousands of leaders in business, the public service, non-profit organizations, community associations, education, and healthcare.

David is the author of three best-selling books: *Becoming Real: Journey to Authenticity* and *Simple Living in a Complex World: A Guide to Balancing Life's Achievements*. He is the co-author of *Accountability: Getting a Grip on Results* (which has sold over 100,000 copies world-wide).

With over 25 years of experience as a family therapist, workshop facilitator, professional speaker, and executive coach, David has developed a unique, personal, and practical approach to transforming leadership at all organizational levels.

David has taught at three universities and has been a faculty member at the Banff School of Management in Alberta, Canada.

JIM REGER

Jim Reger has over 25 years of experience in the information technology industry, both in senior management positions with large multinationals and in a number of information technology start-ups.

As a speaker and facilitator, Jim has delivered seminars to thousands of business owners and their staffs across Canada. Over 850 business owners have attended *Creating Results*, The Reger Group's extensive year-long entrepreneur development program. In addition, over 1500 individuals have graduated from The Reger Group's comprehensive training programs for start-up businesses.

The Reger Group is a family business. Jim and his daughter Natasha facilitate improvement of interpersonal communication skills in family businesses and the establishment and running of effective family council meetings. Together they have worked with hundreds of family businesses in North America and Australia.

About the Interviewees

THIS BOOK IS A RESULT of the perspectives of many people. We have known many for years, but met some for the first time during an interview. Not only are their perspectives a foundation for this book, their authentic lives and exemplary leadership are inspirational.

No matter what their varied roles are, common threads run through their lives. They are committed to *authentic leadership*. In these individuals and in countless other authentic leaders we have met and worked with over the years, due diligence, personal reflection, and regular practices lead to transformation of knowledge into wisdom over time.

NORM AUGUSTINE

Norm is former Chairman and CEO of Lockheed Martin Corporation. He is recipient of the prestigious Pace Award for Ethics in 2005 (an award given to a CEO selected for their commitment to ethical behavior). Norm has served in numerous voluntary positions, notably as chairman of the American Red Cross and president of the Boy Scouts of America.

PETER BLOCK

Peter is an author, speaker, and partner in Designed Learning, a training company that conducts consulting skills workshops. He is author of four best-selling books: *Flawless Consulting: A Guide to Getting Your Expertise Used*; *The Empowered Manager: Positive Political Skills at Work*; *Stewardship: Choosing Service over Self-Interest*; and *The Answer to How Is Yes: Acting on What Matters*. Peter is an authentic leader in all aspects of his life.

DON CALVELEY

Don has a passion for the catering and restaurant business. He is President and CEO of Truffles Group Inc. (TTG) of Victoria, British Columbia, which owns Platinum Destination and Event Management; Habitat (which provides all food services for Royal Roads University); and the Harbour Canoe Club restaurant. Don has received the British Columbia Restaurateur of the Year Award (Casual Dining Category). Don attributes his entrepreneurial success to his belief in building equity in human resources. He invests his time, money, and energy into developing himself and his team.

DON CAMPBELL

Don purchased a ranch in Meadowlake, Saskatchewan from his father in 1980 and now operates the ranch with his sons. Don is actively engaged in consulting and teaching ranchers and farmers in western Canada about the principles and practices of Holistic Resource Management, a revolutionary approach to decision-making and management that considers people, their economics, and the environment as being inseparable. He is a mentor and guide to many, particularly in the area of building strong character.

JOHN CHARETTE

John is semi-retired from OBX (Out of the Box Solutions), in Winnipeg, Manitoba. He is a career public servant who has sustained an authentic presence in public service. For 32 years, he built communication bridges between jurisdictions and public service sectors. John's legacy is that public service and Canada are better today because of his courage, contributions, and passionate commitment to public service.

MIKE CRAPE

Mike is CEO of Crape Geomatics Corporation, a company that maps and surveys well plats and pipelines for the oil and gas industry. Crape Geomatics has a main office in Calgary and 140 staff members in two branch offices.

ROB CROOKS

Rob is manager of Workplace Wellness at Shaw Cable in Calgary, Alberta, where he is accountable for health and safety, wellness, and disability management. Rob has conducted training for an employee assistance program (EAP) provider using workshops and stress management techniques. He now concentrates on disability and safety management.

JIM DEMESA

Jim is a successful physician and now CEO of Migenix, Inc., a biopharmaceutical company that focuses on developing innovative drugs that target life-threatening diseases. Jim lives in Vancouver, British Columbia, Canada. He is the author of *BeHappy! Your Guide to the Happiest Possible Life*, and brings amazing presence to his work as a leader.

TIM DUTTON

Tim is CEO of SCOPE, in Sarasota, Florida. He is well known in Sarasota for his universal hugs, dogged pursuit of broad community engagement, and ability to lead individuals and agencies in cooperative social transformation. Tim has a passion for people and community that has led him from hospital administration in Ohio, to healthcare in rural Haiti, and to social change in Sarasota. When not encouraging people to have conversations that matter, Tim can be found riding his motorcycle, mentoring young adults to follow their heart, or imagining how to add more voices to the community's dialogue.

DOREEN FINCH

Doreen is a 74-year-old grandmother. She is an artist who describes herself as a free spirit, preferring to see things from a different viewpoint. Doreen thinks that art, like life, should be completely unique. She has created farm animals known as Finch's Fairly Funny Funky Folk Animals, and is not concerned about whether people like them or not. Doreen lives in Nanaimo, British Columbia, Canada.

SAM GEORGES

Sam is CEO of Anthony Robbins Holdings, owner of all Tony Robbins enterprises. After spending 4 years the U.S. Air Force, he obtained a law degree and practiced law for 17 years before becoming CEO of a seminar company. As general legal counsel and right-hand man for Tony Robbins for the past 14 years, Sam has acquired a wealth of experience in authentic leadership. He has broadened his personal and leadership development skills through extensive study with mentors Brugh Joy and Richard Moss.

JAMIE GROOMS

Jamie is a co-founder and CEO of AxoGen, based in Gainesville, Florida, and founder and former CEO of Regeneration Technologies Inc. AxoGen is an innovative company created to provide surgeons with biological solutions to repair and regenerate peripheral nerves damaged by injury. He is known for strong leadership and for not being afraid to try new approaches, saying he learns a lot more from his failures than from his "home runs."

KATE HARLING

Kate is a psychotherapist who practices in Berkeley, California. She is a grandmother, mentor, and sage. Kate is a rare, amazing person with an authentic presence and spirit. She touches everyone she meets with her sense of respect for the human experience and her capacity to trust. Spend 5 minutes with Kate and you will be uplifted and inspired.

HAL IRVINE

Hal Irvine, M.D., is a rural family physician and anesthesiologist. He is known in his community as a physician who genuinely cares about patients. His children are grown, allowing him to pursue motorcycling, his new authentic calling in life. Hal lives in Sundre, Alberta, Canada.

DALE KELLY

Dale is CEO of AgraPoint International, Inc., Kentville, Nova Scotia, one of Canada's largest and most comprehensive teams of specialists and associates in the agri-food sector. AgraPoint assists farms and agri-food operations to enhance profitability using specialized production and business services. Dale is an authentic leader who is committed to live by authentic principles and practices.

JEFFERSON C. KNOTT

Jeff has been a marketing executive for a leading multinational healthcare company that operates in over 120 countries, president of a leading U.S. building materials corporation, and international vice president of a start-up furniture retailer that is now the largest furniture retailer in the U.S. Jeff is now Chairman of Tintagel Holdings LLC, presently a private global corporate advisement company. He has lectured on global business development at the American Management Association, the Japan External Trade Organization, the University of South Florida, Stetson and the University of Tampa. He attended Harvard Business School Multinational Marketing Program for Senior Executives and on two occasions was a recipient of the U.S. President's Award for Excellence in Exporting. Jeff is a member of a number of boards, including the Board of Trustees of the University of Tampa and the Dr. K. Patel Foundation for Global Understanding. He is also a member of the Leadership Group, Initiative for Global Development, founded by William Gates Senior.

LEN MARRELLA

Len, founder and president of the Center for Leadership and Ethics, Ltd., is a graduate of the United States Military Academy at West Point. After successful military assignments at NATO and in Vietnam, he returned to academia, earning an MBA and Doctorate in Finance and Management. After 22 years of managing major defense projects for the U.S. Army, he retired with the rank of colonel and began a new career in private industry with International Paper Company as Director of Capital Projects. In this capacity, Len was responsible for the implementation of a $6 billion capital investment program. He was International's chief financial spokesperson to Wall Street and other global financial centers. He is a founding partner of Spring Ridge Financial Group and host of a weekly radio program focused on financial issues.

Len's vision is to inspire and enable professional relationships based on trust. He is the author of *In Search of Ethics: Conversations with Men and Women of Character.*

MARY MARTIN

Mary is an organization development consultant. She assists leaders who are interested in maximizing human potential in their organizations. She teaches in the MALT leadership program (Masters of Art and Leadership Training) at Royal Roads University in Victoria, British Columbia, Canada.

GEORGE MCFAUL

George is an international teacher and senior yoga instructor with certification from the Yoga Association of Alberta, Canada and a member of the International Association of Yoga Therapists and the Association of Massage Therapists and Holistic Practitioners. He has taught Hatha Yoga since 1995 and is a member of the faculty of the Donna Farhi Advanced Yoga Studies Program, an internationally renowned facility. George has an honors BA in Eastern Religions. He is owner and senior instructor at Open Spaces Yoga in Cochrane, Alberta, Canada.

MARY MICHAILIDES AND CAROLINE MISSAL

Mary and Caroline are elementary school principals in Edmonton, Alberta, Canada. They are gifted leaders, teachers, community builders, and authentic individuals who make a difference in their schools and in the city of Edmonton, Alberta, Canada.

STEVE MORROW

Steve is a telecommunications industry consultant with inCode Wireless in San Diego, California, a wireless strategy and technology development company that focuses on emerging wireless technologies and enterprise applications. He has more than 20 years of experience in the telecommunications industry and in senior leadership roles in technology planning and deployment, operations management, business planning, and corporate development. His experience includes 15 years with TELUS, Canada's second largest telecom service provider. He has provided consulting services for Alta Telecom International and Deloitte Consulting. Steve lives in Calgary, Alberta, Canada.

RAY NELSON

Ray is founder and former CEO of Nelson Lumber Ltd. Nelson Lumber is now one of the largest home manufacturing and lumber retail companies in Canada. In December 1999, at age 79, Ray became the oldest person to receive a heart transplant. He received the heart of a 55-year-old donor, which would have gone unused because of the donor's advanced age. Ray's new heart and strength of character live on.

ROB REID

Rob is a sports footwear entrepreneur in Victoria, British Columbia, Canada and owner of three Frontrunners Footwear stores and a New Balance store, with outlets throughout Vancouver Island. His passion is to be of service to his community. He is the founder of Runners of Compassion (a service group of runners that conducts local and global fundraising); Race Director of the Royal Victoria Marathon; Event Coordinator of the Terry Fox Anniversary Event (which commissioned a monument to Terry Fox located at Mile Zero in Victoria); Leadership Chairman for the 2005 United Way; winner of the Chamber of Commerce Business and Business Persons Awards for 2003 and 2004 and the BC Ethics in Action Award for 2005; and a member of the Victoria Community Council Quality of Life Employers' Task Force.

BOB RICHARDSON

Bob is founder and CEO of one of the largest real estate and consulting brokerages in Sarasota, Florida, with more than 30 years of leadership in sales and development. Bob is a community business leader, having served tirelessly in various positions on numerous community and professional organizations. An activist in Civic, Environmental and Children's causes, his passion is to pass on the legacy of a better world through our environment and our children. His philanthropic work reflects his dedication to the betterment of the environment and the community, making him a genuinely authentic leader.

BEV SUEK

Bev is former CEO of the Women's Enterprise Centre of Manitoba, a non-profit organization funded by the Canadian government, which loans money to women who are starting or expanding their businesses. The organization also provides business advice and training for women entrepreneurs and their business partners. Bev has run her own business in human resources consulting for workplace mediation and investigation for 25 years.

MARK SZABO

Mark Szabo is an Account Director at Critical Mass, an international interactive marketing company whose clients include such companies as Mercedes Benz, Nike, Dell computers, and NASA. Mark lives in Calgary, Alberta, Canada.

RAY TAILLEFER

Ray is CEO (retired) of Alta-Fab Structures Ltd., Alberta, Canada. Alta-Fab is a 100,000-square-foot manufacturing facility with more than 250 employees and annual sales over $50 million. Ray is a rare, authentic business founder. Succession in his family business is a celebration rather than a battleground.

JUDY WALTON

Judy is Vice President of Human Resources (Canadian Region) for Conoco Phillips (the fifth largest integrated oil and gas company in the world). She works on global redesign of human resources for Conoco Phillips.

GERALD "JERRY" WEINBERG

Jerry is CEO of Gerald Weinberg & Associates. He is a well-known name in the computing industry and author of numerous books about consulting and all phases of a software project life cycle. He is recipient of the J. D. Warnier Prize and the Stevens Award. He has worked for IBM, Ethnotech, and Project Mercury and has been a faculty member at Columbia University, New York and the University of Nebraska, Lincoln. Jerry is a master teacher, consultant, and community builder.

IAN WEST

Ian is a former CEO of a long-term care facility in Calgary and now President of the Spectrum Group of Companies Ltd., and Vice President, Operations with Park Place Seniors Living Inc. in British Columbia. Ian has an incredible ability to lead with authentic presence.

CHARLES "CHUCK" WILLIAMS

Chuck is an Electrical Engineering graduate of Dalhousie University in Halifax, Nova Scotia. He spent 16 years at Hewlett-Packard Company in various sales, management and executive capacities in Canada, the U.S. and Europe. He was President and CEO of Geac Computer Corporation when it became a public company. Later, he formed a consulting firm and became an advisor, consultant and sometime investor in small, often start-up private companies. In 2003 he retired as Chairman of Oiltec Resources Ltd. of Calgary, Alberta, Canada.

BENNET WONG AND JOCK MCKEEN

Bennet Wong, M.D., F.R.C.P (c) is a trained psychiatrist. Jock McKeen, M.D., F.R.C.P (c) is a practitioner of Eastern and Western medicine. Since retiring from medical practice, Ben and Jock have blended an in-depth approach to self-development aimed at integration of the individual in body, mind and spirit, emphasizing responsibility for the self in health, relationships and lifestyle. Their work is considered pioneering in the field of personal growth and authentic expression. They are founders of The Haven Institute, a licensed residential education center in the Gulf Islands, British Columbia. They are the authors of six books and the subjects of *Ben and Jock*, a biography.

PATTY WOODS

Patty is Workforce Planning Leader at Hallmark Cards, assisting with identification of workforce planning needs. Her responsibilities include keeping the census for the core business and conducting analyses of hiring and turnover rates. She is currently launching a new human resources information system (HRIS) as the lead for documentation, training, communication, and change management.

GERRY ZIMMERMAN

Gerry has been Fire Chief of the City of Kelowna, British Columbia since 1990. He was honored by *Macleans Magazine* in 2003 as a Top Ten Canadian Citizen of the Year. He was instrumental in guiding the City of Kelowna through recovery from a horrendous forest fire in the summer of 2004 that destroyed over 250 homes.

Publisher's Comment

HOW MANY AUTHENTIC PEOPLE do you know? Have you ever worked for an authentic leader? If you were to take all the people you interact with on a personal level (at home, work, school, at your house of worship, the country club or Rotary Club, and even at the grocery store), how many of them are truly "authentic"?

Are you authentic? Are you an authentic leader? What do those around you think?

These may seem to be unfair questions, especially since each of us might have a personally acceptable definition of what an "authentic person" should be. Most likely each of us has a working definition in our subconscious that we have stored away for that very moment when a judgment call has to be made. Someone may ask, "Is that person genuine?" "Are they for real?" Whether we use these exact terms or not, we do make these judgment calls, based on various methods of measurement.

Young people often judge others on such criteria as how well they do in their grades at school; the number of friends they accrue (and retain); if they have the "right" clothing or drive the "right" car; if they bring something unique to the class that enhances its standing within the school; or if others follow their lead. In the same way adults often judge others in the business world: Have they increased sales for the company? Do they demonstrate leadership skills that others do not? Are they creative? Are they cost conscious? Do others follow their example?

If an authentic person enters your life, believe me, you'll know it. You'll recognize him or her for who they are. It may not strike you like a lightning bolt, but in a short period of time you'll recognize them. Likewise, you'll easily recognize the inauthentic person. You may not be schooled in deciphering the differences, but you'll intuitively know the difference between the two. Guess which one you'll most likely gravitate toward?

What David Irvine and Jim Reger present in this book can have a profound effect on you — if you allow it to happen. Those of you who are already authentic leaders will be validated and enhanced by what they share. For those of you who are seeking to become authentic leaders, David and Jim offer realistic, down-to-earth examples, stories, and direction that can produce the results you desire.

Being "authentic" requires a wide range of abilities and skills, talents and personality traits. Each truly authentic leader is as different as roses on the same bush. They are all authentic roses, but each has flair, a specialty, a uniqueness that sets them apart from the others. Similar... different... unique... the same.

Authentic leaders have a sense of who they are. Character is one key component; understanding oneself is another. The personality that others see when they observe us is critical when people assess us as being authentic or not. As the TV commercial states, perception really is everything. How other people assess us will add to or diminish our leadership ability. Since truly authentic leadership comes from within, authentic leaders recognize their limitations, own up to their mistakes, know how and when to ask for help, allow their internal persona to rise to the occasion when needed, and refuse to become entwined with power issues.

An outstanding authentic leader acts as a facilitator, a compass, an encourager. He or she is people focused; a listener who allows discussion and diverse opinions to be heard; one who is willing to express and share feelings openly.

An authentic leader isn't averse to employing the necessary tools at the appropriate time — be those tools a hammer and shovel, a voice and support, or a shoulder — to get something done, without passing the task onto others.

Whether at home, school, work, or in any other environment, an authentic leader is someone who is eager and willing to give credit when credit is due. A leader says "thanks" and shows appreciation for a job well done or an effort well executed.

Inside the covers of *The Authentic Leader*, you will experience some very personal and life affirming stories and examples. The people that were interviewed during the writing of the manuscript are all outstanding examples of what leadership can and should be. Let these stories roll around inside your head. The results could be life changing.

It has been a pleasure to work with David Irvine and Jim Reger to produce this book. May it serve as a compass in your life. Good reading.

*—**Dennis McClellan**, Publisher*

Perspective — The Healing Power of Stories

O UR BELIEF IS THAT PLANETARY HEALING is preceded by personal healing and that for personal healing to occur, one must look inward, searching for wholeness among all the fractured parts.

STORYTELLING

The art of storytelling has been used as a tool for personal and societal transformation for centuries. We find that telling stories about oneself and listening to the stories of others are important instruments for reaching one's authentic self as well as encouraging others to uncover their authentic selves. The very act of telling a personal story to another person is in opposition to the pull toward isolation that is so prevalent in our modern-day world. Storytelling also contains the seeds of an *authentic community* because each person's story could be about any of us. Learning the art of telling stories takes time and patience, but the mere act of telling them is a powerful remedy for a society consumed by efficiency and velocity.

Never has so much information been as accessible as it is today. Yet *perspective* — and the wisdom that emerges from life's experiences and the stories that are heard when sitting face to face with another person — can never be fully experienced on the Internet. Stories told while in the company of another person provide a place of *authentic belonging*. Only when we recognize that the soul's desires will never be fully satisfied in a society that reduces the meaning of life to possessions and material success, do we begin to realize that everything surrounding us is a part of the search for new sources of significance and that we are struggling with some of the same questions that challenged our ancestors.

Fortunately, our ancestors left a trail to follow, dimly discernable at times, but still there all the same. Their stories, like our stories, can lead to a deeper understanding of one's own origin and destination. Stories bring a sense of meaning to a collection of seemingly unrelated random events. At the end of life, all that will be left of us is our story, so within our stories are the seeds of immortality. Knowing that future generations can retell our stories can be liberating, perhaps even leading to a sense of being in a realm of timelessness.

We hope that the stories of our respective journeys to authenticity will provide illumination of *your* story, or the story of someone you care about, and lead you to a deeper recognition and appreciation of your own journey. If you can recognize defining moments in your life more clearly, then weave them into a tapestry of greater understanding, and then turn this understanding (and meaning) into seeds of new growth, our deepest desires will be realized.

JIM'S STORY

It Is Not About Pretense; It Is About Realness.

I do not think that I consciously considered the meaning of authenticity and leadership until I was in my late twenties.

My father's tragic suicide when I was 7 years old forced my mother to work more than full-time to support her three young children. I was left pretty much on my own to figure out my place in the universe.

Thinking back, it is obvious that I made two key decisions at that time. The first decision was that I would never again withstand the pain of having a cherished loved one taken away from me. The strategy I subconsciously employed to accomplish this was to build a "brick wall" around myself, thinking that if I never let anyone get into my heart again, then I would never have to withstand the kind of pain that comes from losing someone I loved. The second decision was that I would not be poor. The stress of not being able to adequately support his family had been a huge factor in my father's departure. So I incorrectly made the assumption that financial security and a happy home life are synonymous.

After my father's death, the next most significant defining moment in my life was the birth of Natasha, my daughter, when I was 28 years old. I can vividly remember questioning myself at the time about what value there could possibly be in having a wall between oneself and one's child — even a wall that was a single brick thick, let alone hundreds! That day my wall came down, and not just a brick at a time — I brought in the bulldozers.

The whole issue of leadership now took on new meaning as it became apparent that the only true meaningful and honest way to demonstrate leadership to my child would be by how I led my life — which led me to question everything about myself. "Who am I really?" and "How will I lead myself so that I can demonstrate to my child things that I hold as important?" became consuming thoughts. They subsequently led me on a never-ending journey to find my real and authentic self. I read, studied, took courses, and pursued every opportunity I could find to learn and to experience more about who I was and what the events of my life and the people in it were meant to teach me. My old beliefs about needing money to have a loving home life were challenged daily as I struggled to find a balance between the time and energy needed for a successful career and the desire to be with my family.

Four years later, the scales were totally tipped in favor of having quality time with my family when my son Brayden was born. Deciding that there would be other opportunities for business ventures, I left a successful career and took my wife and two children to Hawaii. We spent almost a year "hanging out" at the beach. I got to be a kid with my kids during the year before my daughter started school and a new chapter in our lives as a family began. This was a defining year in my life. I realized just how much can be learned from our children. My children were instrumental in helping me gain a solid sense of myself and what mattered most in my life. From this solid grounding, I was able to rebalance my life. From a more secure place, I threw myself into new entrepreneurial ventures, taking along a passion for imparting my authentic self and my family values into my leadership style.

The next 10 years were the happiest years of my life. We grew as a family, and I grew into a more open person, learning to know and love myself at a deeper level, and thereby being able to love and connect with other people more fully. While still passionate about my work, it never consumed me again because I had let go of the notion that my worth as a husband, father, and individual was in any way connected to my net worth.

These years were filled with meditation and a deep spiritual search to find out more about who I really was and then to live my life from this authentic place. It was primarily during this period that I formed a solid basis of meaning in my life and became clearer about my true purpose in life, the principles that I would live by, and the choices that would assist me in creating the results I wanted.

Over the past 20 years I have worked with thousands of entrepreneurs, with the primary focus of my efforts being to assist them in determining what is truly important in their lives, to identify their higher purpose, to find their authentic self, and to integrate this person into how they lead and learn in their businesses, communities, and families.

DAVID'S STORY

That which we are most capable of teaching others is what we are most in need of developing within ourselves.

My life's work has been about "connection." Arriving into a family of helping professionals, I was born to be a therapist. Both of my parents were social workers; my sister became a psychotherapist; and my brother became a physician. I have vivid memories of mediating a fight between my parents when I was 5 years old. I know that this was no great act of altruism — rather it was all about survival. This type of skill came naturally to me. As I grew up, I became a high achiever in anything I pursued, following a path of success and compliance, constantly securing approval from significant adults by being the "good" kid.

Immersion in a fundamentalist religion in my formative years supported my compliant nature. This fundamentalist religion instilled a strong moral sense of right and wrong along with a hierarchical view of life. Although my parents impacted me significantly by their respective transformational quests to move beyond the obedience and authority expected in our religion, the influence of fundamentalism held me firmly in its grip for many years, even after I formally left the church.

I mistakenly thought being polite was living from my heart. Striving for perfection and hiding behind a cloak of caretaking actually masked my fear and insecurity. Sensitivity and compassion ensured my success as a psychotherapist, but all the while I was concealing uncertainty and a need for approval. I was both disconnected from and distrusting of my authentic voice. Often when I was around strong personalities whom I respected, I lost the connection with what really mattered to *me*.

Having over-identified with my parents and my religion, I became a workaholic who was always trying to "get it right." I was a successful family therapist and very helpful to my clients, but I lived in a world of perpetual anxiety for years. I worked 60 to 70 hours a week. I ran marathons at near 6-minute miles, but could not sit still for 5 minutes… for to be alone with myself for any length of time without doing or achieving something created far too much discomfort. I seemed to be skimming along the surface of life, rather than being fully immersed and present to *experience* life.

This lack of a clear sense of an authentic center, along with a propensity toward drastic mood swings (a "gift" I inherited from my father) resulted in severe depressive and manic episodes. The final and most devastating episode culminated in my standing on a highway ready to step in front of a Kenworth semi-truck. At that moment, the thought struck me: *Where does a person go for help if he is the only therapist in town?*

To paraphrase the words of the poet Robert Pinsky, I had found myself midway on my life's journey, in dark woods, the right way utterly lost. Deep down, I knew that only through risk could I fully open my heart. This dark night of my soul, along with its inexplicable anguish, led me to a psychiatrist's office, to years of intense self-discovery, and eventually to the recovery of my authentic self. In due course, this personal darkness helped me find a spiritual program within an authentic community of people who supported me, who had the courage to tell me the truth, and who held me accountable for living an honest life.

Coming face to face with my demons, I began to value honesty and integrity above the old patterns of denial, illusion, and indulgence. By learning to let go of self-will and rely on a power greater than myself, I started to be able to hear a deeper voice from within me. The process of surrendering, along with accompanying habits that support, renew, and align me into this new reality, form the basis of my transformational experience. This authentic journey has positively affected my leadership ability in every area of my life and has been my pathway to inner peace.

Through the development of an internal "rootedness," today I am much less inclined to seek comfort, direction, and security through external — temporary — gratification. I have been able to access a sustained source of clarity, strength, and courage from within. My need to *prove myself to the world* has being transformed into a desire to *express myself in the world*. No longer is life about what I have on the outside. Now it is more about who I am on the inside.

Although I still find great fulfillment in helping others, I left my psychotherapy practice in 1989. Since then I have worked in the leadership development field, helping leaders to find their own unique path to authenticity.

I have learned that I cannot change or heal things that I do not acknowledge, and what I fear, I will create — a sort of self-fulfilling prophecy. I believe that everyone needs teachers on the outside to help us trust the teacher on the inside. I work with many leaders who describe their quest for authenticity as being about a "softening" or becoming more "vulnerable." Yet, because sensitivity has always been my strength, my path has been more about "toughening" and trusting myself. Both are different paths to the same destination. At long last, I am beginning to break free of the instruction of my external teachers into a rhythm of my own. This has enabled me to guide leaders seeking to amplify their impact on the world; to continue to free myself from the approval of others; and to discover, in the process, a deep sense of satisfaction — in work and in all areas of my life.

My quest for identity and a desire for intimacy — which have been a vital part of me for as long as I can remember — fuel my passion for authenticity. I have come to accept both the quest and the accompanying struggle, knowing that it will never be completely resolved. It is this never-ending pursuit that provides fuel for the creative fire burning inside me.

* * * *

CHAPTER 1

—— ⚬ ——

The First Principle —
Authenticity Is Powerful
And Inspirational

*Spiritually evolved people, by virtue of their discipline, mastery
and love, are people of extraordinary competence, and in their
competence they are called on to serve the world, and in their
love they answer the call. They are inevitably, therefore, people
of great power, although the world may generally behold them as
quite ordinary people, since more often than not, they will
exercise their power in quiet or even hidden ways.*
—**M. Scott Peck**

* * * *

THE ULTIMATE PURPOSE OF LIFE IS TO DEVELOP
THE SOUL

David Winestock is a former physician and an internationally rec-
ognized specialist in neuroradiology and neuropathology. Now in
his sixties, David is a welder who volunteers as a high school shop

teacher in Victoria, British Columbia. He no longer practices medicine, but instead practices a trade. He is on a mission to persuade young students that in many cases, there can be no better, no more satisfying calling than working in a skilled trade that produces visual results at the end of the day.

David is the son of a physician and was expected to follow suit. Yet, his greatest passion in school was shop class. His heart was in building things. When practicing medicine, however, he never had time to pursue his passion for building. For David, medicine provided him with little satisfaction. It lacked something that he described as a "God feeling." Shortly after turning 50, David retired from medical practice. He took a welding course and a passion for welding and teaching was sparked. Soon, he signed on as a volunteer and now spends every day teaching.

"I get a huge reward from it," David says. "When Fridays come around, I'm the only person in the school who is upset." David is a man who loves his "job" so much that he dreads Fridays. He is a man who says, "If I weren't happily married, I'd sleep at the school."[1]

David Winestock is on an authentic journey because he has come to grips with the matters of the soul. He understands that the fundamental purpose of life is to develop one's soul by serving other people. Following the matters of one's heart, passions, and gifts nourishes and grows the soul. For David, growing his soul meant walking away from the medical profession.

Pursue Developing the Soul

Developing the soul can have countless forms of expression. Start by making room to reflect on matters of the heart — passions, purpose, inner satisfaction — things that are unrelated to the generation of wealth. Although wealth will undoubtedly provide options, and in some ways make possible the pursuit of matters of the soul, the real work of life is below surface matters such as wealth, eminence, and materialism. Take time to reflect on several questions:

- Have I ever been at work when some part of me did not seem to be there?

- Are there gifts that I do not use, passions that I do not express, or talents that I conceal?

- When my paid work is not in alignment with my true nature, how do I attain fulfillment? (For example, perhaps you have a kind heart, but you work in an environment that is so demanding that kindness is downplayed or even rejected. Maybe you have a unique capacity to guide other people through complex situations, but do not have opportunities to be a mentor. Perhaps you are a gifted storyteller, but cannot use this talent in your chosen career.)

- Have I ever worked in an organization only to find that I have far more talent, creativity, capacity, and resourcefulness than my current job required or even permitted?

- What happens to my soul when my gifts do not seem to have a place in what I am doing?

- What happens when the purpose of my work is eroded by demands of the world? Or when the expectations of others crowd out things that matter most to me, thus leaving my spirit feeling small and brittle, thereby diminishing my soul?

No quick method, no 30-minute values-clarification exercise, will answer these questions. There is no absolute, clear-cut solution to the quandaries that arise from them.

These questions are actually questions of the heart that beckon us to follow a deeper voice than that offered by modern-day culture. Keeping these questions, or our own version of them, firmly in our minds and hearts, having an internal dialogue with them, and inquiring into what the answers might mean; reaching out to others on the journey for support; and remaining curious about the possibilities can lead to things never thought possible with the strategic-planning part of the brain. Those already on an authentic journey know that internal creative fires are fueled by inquiry itself.

The path to nurturing the soul is not linear. Sometimes, moments of being utterly confused and disheartened, and unable to grasp any degree of clarity, occur even in the midst of a quest. Yet, these moments of being lost provide opportunities to simply "sit still" and wait — wait for discovery, wait for clarity, and wait for answers.

Jeff Knott talked of what happens when he is engaged in following his passion:

> I believe in putting my efforts where my true passion is, which is doing something that will provide a service or product or need to human beings on the planet so that I can say I made a difference. When I am doing something I love, my mind keeps going a zillion miles a minute thinking of ideas, implementing them, and providing inspiration to the people around me who share my passion. I'm on the board of one of the leading zoos in the U.S. The people there just love to work with wildlife. For example, I have heard people say, "I don't get paid a lot, but I love what I do. I go home happy and I look forward to coming to work to see my baby chimpanzees!" Yet, on the other hand, I know some great people who make millions of dollars a year — but do they really love what they do?

We find it intriguing that with all Jeff's credentials and leadership positions in organizations around the world, what excites him most is giving back to others, and in being a part of the fulfillment in people's lives in this small, but significant way.

Be "At Home"

Anyone who has traveled knows how it feels to come home. Travelers understand the difference between being "in the world," meeting the demands of society, and being "in a sanctuary" of a familiar place — a chair, a bed, a room, or a garden or yard — where they can take a deep breath and experience the joy of coming home to a familiar, self-nourishing place. Simply connecting with one's soul in this type of sanctuary, without necessarily finding immediate or perfect clarity, leads to finding the way back to a sense of "home" that we knew as children.

In childhood, being "in the world" meant having no plans and no agendas. We simply met the world as it presented itself. This type of being "in the world" is a place of authenticity that poets speak of, a sense of being at home with ourselves no matter where we are and no matter what the world dishes out. As long as we live in a place "away from home," the search for happiness outside of ourselves will continue. The world and all its materialistic allures will never satisfy our search. Inner peace and balance will always be elusive until we come home to a sense of "place" that is within our authentic selves.

Life is actually a journey of "coming home." When engaging in life from a sense of "home," our deepest parts become engaged in everything we do. We do not become tired, but instead find passion and sweet satisfaction for the longings of our spirits, knowing that in this "home" place we are doing what we are *meant* to do in life and in work. From this home place, unique gifts will be discovered, making our world a better place because of our presence. Serving and impacting other people from that deep authentic place within oneself is what we call *authentic leadership*.

A friend once described being "at home" with her own self when she began a new, significant relationship at age 52:

> Having lived alone, as a single parent, for more than 10 years, I didn't *need* a relationship to come home to. I had already found peace within myself. The effect of this was that my world was different because *I* was different. So I'm starting this new relationship without game-playing, posturing, and pretenses. I don't need approval from this man, nor do I fear rejection like I did when I was dating in my twenties. The relationship is real because *I'm* real. This realness brings vulnerability and intimacy to our relationship in a way I've never known before. I didn't seek out this relationship — this relationship just seemed to find me.

Bringing this type of "at home," centered self to a relationship, whether the relationship is with a lover, a job, an organization, or a child, creates a sense of freedom and ease. Although more is risked, not because circumstances make taking risks *seem* safer, risks are taken because there is a sense of greater self-trust. Worry is reduced because fears are lessened. There is less stress and greater relaxation because of the security and sense of worth that come from within as a result of being fully present in life.

The journey to an authentic self is what we call evolution and development of the soul. From this place of "being home" comes the greatest capacity for impact on people we serve. Yet, an authentic journey is not an overnight event, but rather a lifelong process.

Marsilio Ficino, a Renaissance philosopher, spoke eloquently about coming home to an authentic self and about what would be found on the journey: "It is useful for us to search for that region which best suits us, a place where our spirit is advanced and refreshed, where our senses remain thriving and where things nourish us." This may be a physical space, but it is ultimately a quality of the heart. We come to this place when we let go of what we believe *should* be happening, and in so doing discover an awareness of what is *already trying* to happen naturally in our lives. Those who are open to this inner voice will begin to recognize — either from the past or in the present — passions that are calling them, turning points that are leading them, or defining moments that are summoning them.

Listen to Internal Promptings

David Winestock's story was about his experience of discovering his passions and internal voice and bringing his authentic self to the world. Now read Kate's story. She "came home" by going to Africa and listening to her internal voice:

> When I was a child I always dreamed of traveling the world, specifically of seeing Ethiopia. I was born in 1942. My father was killed 3 years later, fighting in the war overseas. Maybe this had something to do with my dream. I don't know where this yearning to travel came from. I only know that it was inside me.
>
> When I was 29 years old, I was a single parent on welfare, and a man wanted me to move in with him. But something inside kept saying, "It's time to go to Africa." This was my first conscious experience of being rubbed up against the culture. You can imagine how all the voices of the world tried to smother my heart's desire. "But you're a single parent. You're on welfare. What are you thinking? Are you crazy?"
>
> The fact is, I had this dream that had to be lived out and nothing was going to stop me. I had worked my butt off for the past 10 years and I just didn't want to go back to living with a man and doing the same thing again. I had

been chief, cook, and bottle washer. I just couldn't go back to more of that. I wanted to see the world. I wanted to have an adventure.

I wanted to go to Africa, but I had no idea how I was going to get there. I also really wanted to go to Israel because I had read all about it and had a fantasy dream about what it was like. So I shipped my stuff to South Africa and then I planned the trip. Of course, we didn't have the Internet in those days, so I just started making phone calls and writing letters. From the phone calls and letters, I found that the best and cheapest way to see Africa and Israel was to fly to Holland, buy a van there, and drive it through Israel to Africa.

So that's what I did. I got on a plane with my 5-year-old daughter, Tracy. I bought a van in front of the American Express office in Amsterdam and drove it through Europe. My romantic self had this idea that I wanted to follow the route down the Red Sea that King Solomon took to see Queen Sheba, the queen of Ethiopia. I was convinced that I could somehow find a boat that would take that van down the Red Sea.

When I got to Israel, I found a guy who was running trips on an Ethiopian fishing boat. He said, "Yeah, we can get your van on the back of the fishing boat." So I made a reservation for 2 months down the road.

Then, because I had run out of money, I went to the Canadian Embassy and asked if they knew of a job for the next couple of months. The embassy people sent me to the First Secretary of the Canadian Embassy, and I moved in there as an au pair and stayed for 2 months.

In my planning for the trip, I didn't know how I would get out of Israel because at the time you couldn't have an Israeli stamp on your passport and then leave Israel to go to any of the surrounding Arab countries. So the big hitch was how to go from Israel to Africa with the van. I had no idea how to get the van out of Israel, but I decided that I would just trust the process. I went on radical faith because I was so determined that I was going to get to live out this dream. No one was going to stop me. I could have left Israel off the list and gone down through the Sahara and driven through Africa, because people were doing that, but I had to pay attention to my heart. And my heart led me in a direction away from what everyone else was doing. I guess that is what you would call authenticity.

There were a whole lot of other little dramas that happened before I got to that fishing boat, but that's how I got to Ethiopia: on total faith.

And where did I get that faith? Who knows? I've asked myself a million times, how come I went in these directions in my life? At that time, I was not in San Francisco getting these ideas. I was in Calgary. There was just something inside me that led me and gave me the trust to follow that voice. Africa was a turning point for listening to and trusting my voice, which set the stage for a confidence to make it in the world. It's what brought me to San Francisco from Canada years ago to start a business on my own. It's what guided me back to a university, and it's what led me to my work today. You have to trust yourself, trust the voice within you, and trust the unknown...

One cannot avoid being touched and inspired by Kate's authentic capacity to trust herself as she stepped continually into the unknown. The source of that trust was her awareness of an unseen force that was guiding her and her willingness to be carried by it.

In our experience, the strength of an internal force is always much greater than we will ever understand. It does not matter what it is called. It does not matter if it is not understood. What matters is that it is there and that it is real. An internal force is something that we can sense if we learn to listen.

For anyone in the work of leading and influencing other people, a vital action is to take time to be alone. Listen to inner promptings. An internal force might say, "No, what needs to happen right now will be found by going in another direction."

The stories told by David Winestock and Kate Harling illustrate the power of authenticity in one's life. In their unique ways, both of these people stood against culture and followed the urge of a deeper internal voice of passion and purpose. Paying attention to one's internal voice, and respecting it, results in an emergence of deeper satisfaction, inner contentment, and greater meaning in life.

The Spanish poet Antonio Machado beautifully expressed listening to one's internal voice and taking a path of authenticity when he said:

You walking, your footprints are the road and nothing else; there is no road, walker; you make the road by walking.

Find the Path

The work of authentic leading begins with authentic *living*, which is finding our own path through life, a path that cannot be limited by anyone else or lived out by anyone else. That path must be taken one step at a time. Seeing a path already laid out far into the distance very likely means that we have stumbled upon someone else's path and need to find our way back to our own path. The path of an authentic journey is always just beneath our feet. If we follow this path, we will recognize that we are in the right place, but probably only *after* we have arrived.

AUTHENTIC LEADERSHIP IN ORGANIZATIONS

Build a Culture that Lasts by Developing Lasting People

Viewing leadership not as a *position*, but as a *presence*, illustrates that your impact can be amplified in any area. Yet, the question still arises: "How can I apply the principles and practices specifically to my work as a leader in an organization?" As so much of our work is focused in the context of the workplace, we devote an early section of this chapter specifically to answering this question. Jamie Grooms comments on how the application of authentic presence can move an organization forward:

> One of my observations is that we have become managers of perception instead of reality. I'm trying to live my life and make my leadership decisions based on reality. When you have empowered people and you communicate the reality about where you are going they understand it and become part of it. There's a connection because we have defined the issues *together* and we understand the philosophies and the outcomes we are trying to achieve. It's about creative energy and a connection where we're all together. And together is the only way to get things done. As a leader, I feel great when I can help people open up doors and find their strengths and then give them a pathway to use them.

In an increasingly tight labor market, corporate culture is becoming an important employee attraction and retention tool. Yet, our research, experience, and observations tell us that many organizations miss the boat by not creating a corporate climate that responds to the changing workforce. Before continuing our discussion, consider the comments of Steve Morrow. He expresses well, in his experience with a company he recently left, the cynicism we see in organizations:

> Companies today, especially those that are publicly traded, are increasingly forced to take a short-term view. Executives are highly motivated to hit quarterly targets in order to influence the share price. Their compensation is based on how well the stock does. In the short run, they end up looking only for ways to cut expenses, which often starts with cutting development. Leaders become glorified politicians who are simply after the next vote and popularity...
>
> Short-term thinking pushes them into making decisions that compromise long-term effectiveness and success of the organization. For example, take front-line engineers. We ask them to build-out our network infrastructure. They tell managers that in order to build this capability into the networks, "We need $2 to $3 million of capital funding to do this properly so it won't break down and it will support new services." But the executives chop it because they don't have the capital. And why don't we have the capital? Because we are trying to hit quarterly cash flow numbers.
>
> The front lines say they are trying to run a race with one leg while having one arm tied behind their backs. In a publicly traded company, the salaries and bonuses of the five highest-compensated executives are published in the

annual report. As soon as the annual report comes out, it's plastered all over the bulletin board. When the executives are getting in excess of $1 million as salaries, when employees haven't been given raises for 4 years, it's a breeding ground for cynicism and negativity.

Every day front-line staff members are becoming increasingly disengaged and cynical about management and leadership. They say, "At our company of 25,000 employees, if we were told we were downsizing and that we had a voluntary package with a year's salary, 20,000 of us would take it and walk tomorrow."

As outlined in earlier sections, everyone in an organization with problems like these shares in the problem *and* in the solution. Positional leaders must make fundamental changes in their workplaces to attract and retain the best people. People on an authentic journey will no longer tolerate compartmentalized lives, giving up core values to keep their jobs or being used as commodities. Organizations with a failing grade in developing cultures that align the purposes, passions, and unique talents of employees with their organizational strategy will soon begin to pay the price. The workplace is rapidly moving into a seller's market, meaning people are growing increasingly intolerant of cultures that are not engaging and do not support their authentic development. Following an authentic path is recognizing that work *can* and *should* provide opportunities for personal growth as well as financial growth. If it does not, we are wasting too much of our lives on it.

The Changing Face of Business

Traditionally, primary stakeholders in a business (owners, employees, and customers) define their "wants." Consider these questions and answers, and reflect on the changing face of business just in the past decade:

- *What do employees want?* To be fairly compensated, a fair business bargain, a fair day's pay for a fair day's work

- *What do customers want?* To receive fair value

- *What do owners want?* To get a fair return on their investment

For organizations to excel and thrive in the future, they must go beyond these traditional "wants" by viewing their culture, their employees, and their customers through the lenses of authentic action.

Today, *employees* want more than fair pay. They want to "belong" and to be honored, valued, and respected as unique individuals. *Customers* want more than fair value. They also want to be valued, appreciated, and respected. *Owners* want more than a fair return on their investment. They also want to enrich the lives of their customers, employees, communities, and families. They want to leave a legacy.

Today, a well-run, sustainable organization needs two sets of measurements for accountability: one for performance and one that is able to align organizational values with the values of the people in the organization. Hanging a mission statement and corporate values policy on the wall has never cut it. As never before, people are leaving dysfunctional organizations. A thirst for power and greed, accompanied by an obsession for efficiency, pushes authentic people, often the most capable and creative people in an organization, out the door.

Courage Is the Solution

The solution for a dysfunctional workplace is having courageous, authentic leadership — men and women who bring their personal values to the office and who are willing to courageously and openly discuss corporate dilemmas and honestly seek feedback, input, and direction from "below." When honesty and integrity and loyalty are embodied in actions of accountability, not only is this good for people who want to be authentic; it is also good for business. Searching for authentic meaning, engagement, and fulfillment has an ability to transform and sustain a business culture.

Changing an Organization Begins Inside

Building a successful and sustaining workplace environment starts "inside." As we will discuss throughout this book, changing the soul of an organization begins with a commitment to developing your personal soul. Next, as positional leaders, we must develop an ability to take our new self-awareness into actionable results in the workplace.

Facilitate Conversation

You will learn in discussions and reflections throughout this book that leadership today can be percolated down to one word: conversation. Before we discuss how to bring renewed conversation to an organization that will lead to renewed action and accountability, read Tim Dutton's description of an authentic workplace culture and authentic conversation:

> One of the conversations we have inside this organization is that we think that we can get done whatever we want to get done if we're willing to allow somebody else to take credit for it. We try really hard to operate under that approach. The first four words of the mission of this organization are "to engage the community." An engaged community is one in which people have a sense of personal ownership and personal connection to what they think matters to that community. Those kinds of

communities tend to be the communities where good things happen — where there's less crime and less cardiovascular disease and even fewer colds. At least that's what the research shows us.

So the organization that I'm directing is a little bit unusual in that it's not so much focused on "How do we solve problems?" as "How do we create a venue around which people in the community can increase their sense of connectedness and network and sense of personal ownership and accountability?" I've got a group of wonderful young people working here and I'd like to think that we feed off each other.

This kind of organization may seem more likely to occur in a community that's reasonably wealthy, but this kind of conversation works well in *any* kind of community. We're funded a little bit by a lot of people, a little bit by the government, a little bit by foundations and the United Way, and a little bit by corporations. That's on purpose as well. We don't want to be beholden to anybody.

In the context of an organization, leadership implies expectations that certain results are to be achieved. Therefore, to complete the cycle of leadership, we must make a transition from having a clearly understood commitment, and to having a clear accountability process for following through on our commitment.[2] Commitment is required in leadership, just as engagement in conversations about our commitments is vital in an organization. Think about these questions: "Does my current leadership invite people to speak about commitments to their dreams, gifts, and passions? Does my presence invite conversations about the need to align one's gifts to the needs of the organization for which I am accountable?"

We can offer some suggestions to assist you in facilitating these conversations:

Support inspiration. Chuck Williams reminds us of an old adage: "Success belongs to the group; failure belongs to leadership." He is adamant that results must be supported by a culture of inspiration:

> A primary function of a leader, in my opinion, is to inspire. I want to look up to a leader and say, "This is the kind of person I want to emulate." I want to view myself in the same way that I view a leader. And that leads me to think about honesty, respect, and dignity as key leadership qualities that have inspired me. Inspiration is from *who* a leader is, not *what* kind of leader they are. It's not about being a cheerleader. That's not what I'm talking about. What I'm talking about is from an *inner standpoint.* I want to emulate what they're doing.

Focus on accountability. Judy Walton describes leadership as "a lot less about style and personality and a lot more about an honest commitment to holding something important." She continues:

> A useful question I ask, to help people stay focused, is, "What do you want me to hold you accountable for?" Some people are a little vague about their own accountabilities. One of the things that I can help with is reminding them and holding them accountable for actions they say they want to take, goals they say they want to achieve, or commitments they have taken on.
>
> It reminds them that they said it was important to them and that I'm going to help them meet their commitments because they said it was important to them. I define something as being important if it's in accord with

their values, goals, highest aspirations, and commitments.

This requires courage of conviction and a bit of a leap of faith to act in ways that are congruent with my internal compass.

Remain true to being authentic. Rob Reid expresses his view of authenticity in a different, but still very specific, way by saying:

I can't step into a weekly confessional and get a total check-up regarding being authentic, but if I'm authentic it builds and builds — like steps on a slope leading to a great peak. As I do things to be true to myself, to really listen and follow my voice, in spite of what the world expects from me, I end up being higher at the end of the day, with the right people around me and the right view.

Never give up. Mary Michailides and Caroline Missal are two leaders in education who are very specific about how authenticity applies in a school:

When we talk about being "relentless" in working with our kids, we mean making a difference. It's like the commercials on TV about the "push, pull, or drag sales." Well, you know what? When it's May and we're going into June, it's not over. We need to do whatever we can to push, pull, or drag our kids over the finish line so that they can get everything they need to successfully go into next year. So there is no end really.

Be honest and respectful. One of our clients, a CEO, describes the challenge to being an authentic leader and being honest, but still respectful, by saying:

It's a world without any acting. If I tell the truth, I don't have to remember what I said. An authentic approach is not being abrasive or confrontational. I try to be clear and consistent and factual so I'm the same all the time. Sometimes people say, "You can't say that to the boss" or "You shouldn't do that!" Why not just tell the truth?

Develop Commitment Conversations

The focus of our work and this book is to convey the meaning of being human in a leadership role. It is our desire to see people have more power and presence by "being more of themselves" — by growing their souls, and in turn, providing support and encouragement to the people entrusted to them.

Consider what Tim Dutton says about conversations that lead to commitment:

> Action doesn't happen without conversation. Conversation is a springboard for change, for transformation. Questions are a powerful tool. Quality conversations happen by using powerful questions.

> The real struggle is about how to get people to the table whose voice hasn't been heard very often... these are conversations that matter.

> We use questions to facilitate conversation about race and culture relations in our company. Historically, our workplace is made up of people from segregated communities. In a session, we posed this question to an African-American man about his sense of personal accountability: "What are you doing or failing to do that contributes to the issue of racism in your community?"

Suddenly, a light bulb seemed to go off for him. He said, "Oh, my goodness. I mentor African-American males and I tell them point blank, because I thought it was helpful, that they won't get a fair shake from the white community here. Now I realize that by telling them that, I'm perpetuating a system that needs to be changed."

This conversation was an epiphany for him.

ENDNOTES

1. Roy MacGregor. 2005, March 14. *Globe and Mail* (newspaper article).

2. David Irvine, Bruce Klatt, and Shaun Murphy. 2003. *Accountability: Getting a Grip on Results*. Calgary, Alberta, Canada: Bow River Publishing.

* * * *

CHAPTER 2

The Second Principle — Presence Is More Powerful Than Position

In everyone's life, at some time, our inner fire goes out.
It is then burst into flame by an encounter with another
human being. We should all be thankful for those people
who rekindle the inner spirit.
—Albert Schweitzer

* * * *

THE PURPOSE OF LEADERSHIP IS TO INSPIRE AND SUPPORT OTHER PEOPLE

In _Les Misérables_, Victor Hugo calls attention to the immense struggles of the soul, the balance of good and evil in human beings, and the continual challenges to the conscience. In a touching scene, Jean Valjean had just been given a new lease on life by the very bishop from whom he stole. Valjean was overwhelmed by the bishop's for-

61

giveness. No one had ever given him a break before: "He told me that I have a soul. How does he know?"

The Role of Leadership

Everyone with a leadership role has an opportunity, perhaps even a *responsibility*, to inspire and support other people on a path to authenticity. Our premise is that the work of awakening and developing souls is not reserved for religious leaders or spiritual mentors. We see the ultimate purpose of leadership as finding and following one's own authentic voice and then inspiring and supporting other people to find and follow theirs. If you want to energize, engage, and focus others to live at their full potential, if you want to inspire deep trust and internal commitment, thereby attracting and retaining the best people, if you want to build an enduring organization, community or family, this is the kind of values-aligned leadership that is required today. In order to accomplish this, first consider this notion: The people you lead are often their own best guides. With that in mind, how do you help them to be true to their authentic selves? First, *show* them how by the way in which you live your life. If you are perceived as living with authenticity, meaning committed to following your soul's calling and then living in accord with your highest values and guiding principles, you will inspire others. Second, *encourage* them to listen to their inner guidance system.

Consider an example of inspiring and guiding one back to their authentic self that occurred with David's nine-year-old daughter, Chandra. She was crying one evening from stress she was feeling at school. In short, she has two very close friends, and when she plays with one, the other is left out. When she plays with the other, the first is left out. When all three play, *she* is left out. For the better part of an hour, in between the sobs, David simply held her while continuing to explore with her the fundamental question of authenticity and then asking, "Chandra, what does your *heart* say?"

She did not find perfect clarity, and the anguish of the situation could not be erased in a few "efficient" minutes. Because Chandra knew that her parents were supporting her on her own authentic journey, and she also knew that her answers would come from within her own self, her parents were able to engage in this type of conversation with her. They were committed to growing her soul because they were also committed to their own authentic journeys.

What Leadership *Really* Is

We have interviewed many influential leaders in preparation for this writing project (e.g., a fire chief who led a community through the worst forest fire in the history of the community, CEOs who are building amazing cultures within their companies, physicians, principals, therapists, world-renowned consultants, and entrepreneurs). Yet, no title or accomplishment has made these people great leaders. Their great leadership comes from having an ability to touch the lives of others, perhaps only one person at a time. If you have never had positional leadership responsibilities, but have helped another person find and listen to their authentic voice, at the end of the day, you have been a great authentic leader. If you have helped even one person to listen to and trust their own authentic voice, are you an authentic leader? Unequivocally, the answer is yes.

Leadership is not a position. Leadership is not a title. Leadership is not personal accomplishment. Leadership is a *presence*, a commitment and a capacity to encourage, support, and guide other people through the strength of who they *are*.

Think about a leadership role you have. It could be in the workplace, as a volunteer in the community, or as a parent at home with your children. Honestly answer, "What do I ultimately desire from this relationship?"

If the response is, "I am here to get the job done and to produce the results that are expected from me," then you are engaged in *management*, not leadership. There is nothing wrong with good management. Good management is imperative for survival in any organization and in any relationship in which tasks and results are required. Yet, deciding to *lead* is making a decision to have a different purpose and to work to achieve a different result. Although the purpose of living is to grow and develop one's own soul, the purpose of leading is to grow and develop the souls of the people one leads.

Developing Leadership

Leadership can be compared to gardening. No plant ever grew faster because a gardener demanded that it do so or because the gardener threatened it. Plants grow only when the conditions are right and they receive proper care. Creating the best environment for plants and for people requires providing continued attention and investment.

Gardeners improve by taking better care of their plants. Leaders improve by learning how to better take care of and love the precious lives they have been given to lead. An environment that nurtures one's own soul can nurture other people's souls. Good gardeners can tell us how to grow beautiful plants. They can simply cultivate an environment that allows a rose to be the very best expression of its own self-beauty. Cultivating an environment that nurtures other people is authentic leadership at its finest.

Judy Walton conducts leadership development programs for senior executives. She said the following about leadership:

> First and foremost, the people at work are still people. Even though in organizations we don't always spend a lot of time talking about people as whole beings, they are just that. And when they are at work, we often see only a facet or a dimension of who they are as whole beings. Try to remember that there are always other things

going on that we don't see. Often it's a gift to them and to the organization if we try to remember that people have interests and aspirations and abilities that aren't always what they bring to work.

Another useful thing to remember in organizations when inevitable conflict arises is that we don't know what's going on in someone's life that might be impacting who they are at work on a given day.

Much of my coaching with senior executives is simply to give them an opportunity to have dedicated conversations that are about them and about improving their capacity as leaders. This dedicated time can take different shapes and directions, depending on the individual, but they seem to value the time that is reserved to focus on them because most of their time is spent focusing on other people and other issues. I think that leaders need this kind of support and dedicated attention that's sometimes hard to find in an organization... not in a remedial way, not in an "always-fix-a-problem" way, but out of a spirit of deep commitment to their success. At the heart of it all, and maybe this is connected to what is called "authenticity," is living life from an orientation of commitment to other successes beyond what we see at the surface... It's a choice that we can make, day-to-day, moment-to-moment, conversation-to-conversation, about how we're going to relate to any person in any situation.

This type of commitment to grow and develop others can find its way into a myriad of human expressions of leadership.

David's seventh-grade daughter, Hayley, recently spoke to him about a boy who was constantly being ridiculed for crying at school. He was the brunt of extensive and pervasive bullying. The family discussed the situation at great length and talked about how easy it is to get seduced into the cultural norms, into the mainstream, popular way of thinking, to the point where your own values and principles become eroded. Later, when Hayley stood against the "culture" and compassionately took this boy aside in search of what was really going on, she discovered that his mother was dying from cancer. She had a personal commitment to stand tall with this boy and respectfully support him, while risking some of her own popularity and need for approval. She exercised authentic leadership at its finest — leadership that is committed to the growth of the soul.

Hal Irvine, a physician, spoke to us about authentic leadership from his perspective. Though he would not describe himself as an "authentic leader," he has a commitment to his patients and demonstrates authentic leadership:

> An "authentic response" would have to do with being committed to my patients, developing relationships with them and listening to what they say to find out what they want and what their illness or symptoms mean to them. It would be working with them at this level rather than just giving them directions about what they should do. My patients feel better about this approach. They feel like I understand them and that they are getting better care. It's the relationships I have with my patients that make the job what it is.

Regardless of our position or role in life, from time to time we are called upon to reach for something deep inside ourselves or inside other people which is a commitment to helping others grow their souls. This is the heart of authentic leadership.

POWER: PRESENCE VS. POSITION

Much of current material about leadership focuses on the external and how leaders can master their resources and achieve deliverable results. Exterior outcomes are important, but defining leadership solely by techniques and an ability to produce measurable results misses a central question about leadership: What is the essence — or the spirit — of leading? What is the basis of achievements and making connections to other people? Leadership is more than what we do. Leadership is something, somewhere, inside leaders. Leadership is not a title. It is a unique, authentic expression of who we are.

Great leadership cannot be reduced to techniques. Great leadership comes from a person's authentic presence — their identity and personal integrity. Authentic leaders are dedicated to understanding who they are, having the courage to be that person, and then inspiring, supporting, and encouraging other people to discover and express their unique, often hidden, talents. The most compelling leadership quality is *who they are*: their core values and leadership passions, which are anchored by strong principles that enable them to face the world with a consistent outlook.

Authentic leadership is a never-ending work in progress that requires a continuous, lifelong commitment to acquiring maturity and self-understanding. Leaders must do more than constantly upgrade their skills. Time must be taken to continually examine their values, beliefs, attitudes, philosophy, and outlook on the world. The greatest power is in their personal vision, which is communicated through the example of how they live their lives daily.

Vision, in this context, is intensely personal. It is a hard-won outcome of dedicated self-reflection: "What do I care about?" "What do I stand for?" "What do I desire most in this world?" "How have I changed for the better?" "What is the source of my courage?" "What legacy am I leaving?" "What is my higher purpose?" The core of great, sustained, life-enhancing leadership is having a connection to one's authentic self. It depends on a commitment to knowing self and thereby framing issues correctly, i.e., answering, "What is really going on, inside me and around me?" Leaders who know themselves and understand their environment are more able to respond with appropriate authentic actions in the context of a situation.

How Do I Find the Answer to "Who Am I?"

Reflecting on people who have walked the path of authenticity *before* you is a powerful way of finding the authentic self *within* you. One of the questions we asked our interviewees was to think about people in their lives who impacted them through the strength of their authentic presence. Consider the responses of two of them.

Chuck Williams told us, once again, how much he admired Bill Hewlett (a founder of Hewlett Packard). Bill occasionally joined the HP-Europe management team in late-night poker sessions and weekend ski trips when he was in Europe for strategy meetings:

> Bill is a person who touched me enormously, not only for his formidable intellect, but primarily for his honesty and integrity. He is straightforward (at times blunt), but completely fair and respectful in his dealings with all of us. I look to Bill with absolute confidence. What he says, I can believe and become a part of.

Dale Kelly told us about Denis Waitley and the power of his presence:

> I met Denis a few times in the early 1990s. The first time was in Minneapolis when he was giving a keynote address to thousands. I was invited to an hour-long meeting with him prior to this address. When we walked

to the stage together, Denis never once took his eyes off me while we talked. I could sense his authenticity and sincere engagement. His eyes seemed to bore through me. I could easily see his compassion and interest in what I was saying. I was impressed at his focus, given the fact he was about to go on stage.

The next time, I had invited Denis to Moncton, New Brunswick, where he gave four presentations in one day. The first stop was a high school. He spoke for about 45 minutes to a group of about a thousand teenagers from grades 9 through 12. They had been pretty fidgety throughout his talk. About halfway through he just stopped, stood quietly and then whispered words something like, "I haven't captured your attention yet... but you are the most important people in this room." I marveled at his ability to read the audience and then confidently work them into his message. At the end of his talk, he received a standing ovation. I had to wait for over an hour while he signed autographs.

Our second stop was at a Chamber of Commerce business luncheon. It was sold-out and he received another standing ovation.

That afternoon Denis spoke at another high school. It was a repeat of the experience he had that morning.

Later in the afternoon, he rested a short time before giving his fourth talk — for an hour and a half. Although Denis was exhausted, and the evening session was toned down a bit from the earlier presentations, he still gave 100% plus. Everyone he met received his undivided attention. I knew then he was authentic — the real thing.

There was no false façade about his approach — he simply believed in people and loved them.

Some people call Denis a "motivational" speaker, which in a sense he is, but what I value most is his genuine quality of being human. He is real, authentic, and focused, and he never loses sight of an audience whether it's large or small.

At this point, think about a person who has had an impact on you — someone who made a difference and altered the course of your life, e.g., a parent or grandparent, a boss, a mentor, a friend or life partner, a colleague, or a child. Recall the nature of that relationship, and the role this person played in your life. Regardless of the role, our premise is that this person did not impact your life because of their techniques or titles. It was something deeper, something more substantial that had impact. This person made a difference by the strength of their *authentic presence* — providing leadership simply by being their own true self. Authentic leadership is when an authentic presence is brought to others.

Leadership Is Presence, Not Position

Manifesting an authentic presence is revealed by "authentic" moments. The effect we have on other people is from the strength of our *presence*, not the power of our *position*. Leading is a personal choice to influence other people by the way in which we conduct our lives from moment to moment. Consider some examples of presence, and the effect of presence on a person's life. The first is Patty Woods speaking of one of her teachers:

Amby Burfoot once won the Boston Marathon. He was my sixth-grade teacher and he had a huge impact on my life. I was one of seven kids. I had loving parents, but with seven kids it was hard for our parents to give us individual attention. One time, Mr. Burfoot pointed out my leadership characteristics. He introduced me to the term *joie de vivre* — joy of life. I had never heard this term or the concept before, but it was as if he had just shone a spotlight on a quality that defined me; instantly I knew what he was taking about.

Next is a story from a CEO about the impact that both his father and his children have on him:

My father, who was a farmer, was terrific at encouraging me to dream. He believed that children are able to accomplish so much when not restricted in reality. They live in a world of fantasy that brings out their best ideas and allows the rest of the world to have all these great inventions. As adults, we harvest the fruits of a child's dream. I see that in the children around me and it encourages me to keep dreaming.

Our third example is about Mark Szabo, an executive who oversees international account management teams. He considers *trustworthiness* to be vitally important for an authentic presence:

I meet with clients several times a year. Account management means integrating other agencies that work with the same client on projects. Enormous credibility and trust have to be earned very quickly. Of course, competency must be dependable, and 100% rock solid, which goes without saying.

People want to know exactly where they stand. There's no room for guessing whether or not I'm being straightforward and giving them the whole picture. It's easy to be seduced into telling people what they want to hear, but if you don't have the courage to tell them the truth, you just won't last as their account manager.

But building trust requires something else, something more intangible. Aside from the obvious need to be a conduit for reliable information and competence, there's also a fundamental relationship quality. Other people have to "buy in" to you as a professional and as a person. They have to connect with you and you have to connect with them. The thing they are drawn to is that you have the courage to be honest, real, authentic, and appropriately vulnerable. You can't be too "corporate" or they won't trust you or want to work with you. You have to let them see who you are, which allows them to like you, not just respect you.

To bring out this authentic quality, you have to know yourself. You have to invest in your own personal development, to learn about yourself, which enables you to objectively observe yourself, to see and experience what actually works, for you and for others. When you are being someone that you're not, you must have a sense that you're "wearing the wrong shoes" *before* other people do. You have to be like a finely tuned instrument. If you're just "playing a role" instead of being yourself, they'll "smell you out," and you won't last.

The quality of realness that compels people to connect with you also enables you to have more clarity and the courage to tell the truth — to sustain your integrity when you'd rather take the easy road and tell a client what they want to hear to avoid the discomfort of telling the truth. It allows you to be confident when you open up to others.

Mark does not just bring authenticity to his work to be successful. Authenticity is not a means to an end. His authenticity is a *result* of his quest to know and understand who he is, which brings meaning and clarity to his life. He is successful because he strives to be a better person. People are drawn to his genuineness, humanness, and commitment to serve them. They are drawn to a quality of trust that is a manifestation of authenticity.

Your title or leadership role is merely a tool — a means — to make a difference in your commitments. Making the decision to lead means that you are now a steward, holding "in trust" the people that you lead, regardless of whether they are employees, community volunteers, young people, a political constituency, or a family. Leading is about earning credibility, trust, and respect from people you lead to fulfill an accountability that has been entrusted to you.

Our final example in this section is about Dr. Lois Hole, co-founder of Hole's Greenhouses, a well-known horticultural business in Alberta. Lois was a successful businesswoman, philanthropist, social activist, author of 14 best-selling books on gardening, a school Trustee, a member of the Order of Canada, and Chancellor of the University of Alberta. In 1999, the Prime Minister of Canada appointed Lois as Lieutenant Governor of Alberta. Yet with all her titles, her leadership was not a result of her *positions*. Her leadership was a result of her *presence*. Like beauty, words cannot describe this essence. Lois was described by the strength — and impact — of her presence, which was her authentic *connection*. Her younger son Jim once said:

> Mom was famous for her hugs. You sometimes get hugs from people when you know it's a formality or something, but with Mom, it was genuine. I think she hugged many dignitaries that maybe she shouldn't have because

of protocol, but she just kind of ignored protocol at times.

Her older son Bill also described his mother's genius about human nature:

> She understood that there was a "cylinder" that people have and that she could invade it and then capture a person's focus by getting inside of that cylinder — and her hugs did that.

Lois said, "I have faith in a better future because I have faith that most human beings want to do the right thing. If we can put aside differences of ideology, if we can learn to love one another, then one day we will enjoy a world where no one needs to live in fear, where no one needs to go hungry, and where everyone can enjoy a good education, the fellowship of friendly neighbors, and the security of a world at peace with itself at long last."

Lois Hole had an authenticity that was manifested in her sense of compassion, her humanity, and her courage to stand by her principles, which she used in her leadership role. Yet, her role did not make her powerful. Her role was merely a tool for expressing her presence. Lois probably did not view herself as authentic or even as a leader. She simply did what she loved to do and, in the process, had an amazing impact on thousands of people with her presence.

Some Final Thoughts

Reflect on the following questions:

- Who has made a difference in my life through their authentic presence?
- How is authenticity expressed in *my* life and in *my* leadership work?

- What do authentic moments, when I am connected to my true self and voice, feel like?

- When was I on the "receiving end" of an authentic connection? What does it feel like when I know other people are connected to their true selves? What impact does this have on me?

- What is the difference between an authentic connection and when someone tried to lead me *in*authentically?

PRESENCE VS. PRESSURE

Think again about another leadership experience you have had. You had an honest, sincere desire to assist a person to take some action. Yet, when you applied pressure, the results were counter to what you wanted. Pressure usually weakens your impact as a leader. Consider a family meeting at David's house:

> One night, during our weekly family council session, I made a "leadership" announcement. I wanted our family to become more "spiritual." So I gave a leadership lecture (skillfully, I thought) about how we would do this. The plan was clear, with unambiguous instructions and even some mandates. After all, I was taking on the "responsibility" of being a good leader at home. Guess what the reaction was? Absolute silence. Everyone was gracious (or maybe scared by my "positional authority" as a father?). At least they pretended to listen to me for most of the speech. Afterward, all their heads were down, waiting for the next item on the agenda.
>
> Later that night, Val gently made a suggestion about spiritual leadership at home. "You might be better off trusting that your influence from *living spiritually* in our

home will have a much deeper impact on everyone than *preaching* about spirituality. Just keep being a *light* rather than a *judge*. Remember that you teach that presence is more powerful than pressure."

In the coming weeks, I shifted my focus from *promotion* of spirituality to *attraction*, simply living qualities of the spirit — honesty, compassion, integrity, service, and respect — and taking emphasis off pressuring the family to live my virtues. I stayed engaged in maintaining discipline — daily prayer; quiet time at night for inviting spiritual connections and making room for moments of wonder, grace, and conversations that center around reliance on a higher power; and faith stories with sources of inspiration — and was also respectful of where other family members were. By doing those things, I was able to "*Be* that change I want to see in others around me." Respect on all fronts grew accordingly.

The distinction between *pressure* and *presence* is in the difference between *power* and *strength*. Power comes from *position*. Power is not being open and transparent, but being closed, attempting to control others in order to find control within oneself. In the story above, David had this experience. Power may get the job done, but power is a source of fear. Fear results from power. Fear will never sustain a relationship or the vitality in a relationship. Power — or pressure — will not sustain commitment and engagement. Bev Suek astutely describes power:

> What I see from people who abuse their authority is mostly a lack of self-esteem. They need to have power over other people and to be seen as having power over other people, using and even misusing it. Having power from "within" as opposed to having power "over" is real-

ly crucial in a leader. There's a real difference between these two things.

Therefore, *strength* comes from *presence* — the vulnerability, realness, and authenticity of a person. It comes from inside, not from trying to control the world, but from accepting the world and working with it. People who have a presence of strength tend to have the respect of others.

Numerous unique ways bring a sense of strength to leadership. Some leaders have an authentic presence and strength from having a capacity for compassion and principled actions. Others have an authentic presence from having a commitment to *loyalty* and *integrity*. Ray Nelson spoke about Nelson Lumber as being a principle-centered company since its early beginnings in the late 1940s. Ray told of a time when a thousand houses were being built in Regina and the economy took a plunge. Many builders simply walked away, but Ray decided to fulfill their corporate responsibility to employees, suppliers, customers, and the communities. Nelson Lumber finished those homes and absorbed millions of dollars in losses.

Strong authentic presence that results from integrity means choosing to do the *right* thing over the *easy* thing. Losses can be gains. According to Ray, "I believe that people want self-fulfillment. It is good to have money and the things it can buy; but it is good to thank God and check around every once in a while to make sure I haven't lost the things that money can't buy."

Presence is a way of *living one's life*, a way of being, and it is a lifelong process. Presence provides leadership naturally from an internal foundation of authenticity. Techniques can never compensate for presence and authenticity.

The strength of presence over the power of pressure comes from an internal source, not trying to control everything, but accepting things as they are and working with them. This includes a willingness to share whatever comes along — sadness, insecurity, intimacy — while still providing leadership by being authentic and standing up for what one knows is the right thing to do.

LEADING VS. LEADERSHIP

For simplicity and familiarity, we use "leadership" and "leading" synonymously. Yet, there is a vital distinction. Leading means stepping up to the challenge when we are needed or asked to do so, but at other times, leading is letting go of our involvement altogether. Jerry Weinberg compares leading to dancing:

> Leading on a dance floor, like leading in life and work, is necessary from time to time, but a dancer knows that to be good, you need to practice leading, following, and sometimes getting off the dance floor altogether. Just because one person leads more often than another doesn't necessarily make them a leader... To be *seen* as a leader — but pretending not to have any selfish motives — is actually being selfish. It's okay to be selfish. There's nothing wrong with that. We're all selfish, but pretending you're not selfish is not being authentic.

> People can sense if your motive for leadership is self-centered, and their natural tendency is to resist. We might want to work together and we might need leadership to jointly accomplish things, but when the endeavor is only to be the leader, we tend to not want to follow. If you have positional power over people, they might follow you out of fear or obedience, but resistance will emerge somewhere. You invite defiance whenever you *impose* yourself as a leader on other people.

Our experience has been that people who *aspire* to be leaders by seeking a position that gives them a mandate and the power to order people around are not authentic leaders. While these kinds of leaders tend to repel others, leaders who are viewed as *not* seeking their leadership role are compelling. Soon after Pope Benedict was elected the leader of 1.1 billion Catholics, he said: "It felt like a guillotine was coming down on me when it appeared I might be elected Pontiff. I prayed to God to be spared, but evidently this time He didn't listen to me." This kind of humanness is not from a person who is actively *seeking* leadership, but from a person who is *willing* to lead — and it is attractive. Conversely, people who are motivated to lead by a desire to be *seen* as a leader invite suspicion, particularly when they say, "I'm doing this for you. I'll lead you to do better things. It's in your best interest to go along with me."

One of the tasks of the authentic journey is to move away from dependency and obedience to external authority and move towards authority on the basis of your own evaluations, judgments, and acceptance of responsibility. Authentic leaders are committed to supporting and encouraging others to do this. We perpetuate *in*authenticity by maintaining dependency and obedience to authority figures.

Some Final Thoughts

Good managers who know how to manage others and get a job done certainly have a place in leadership, but that is not the kind of leading we have been talking about. Regardless of how skillful one is at coercing, mandating, and manipulating people to do things from the power of a position, if the goal is to build mutual respect, engagement, and lasting commitment, ordering people around is not the type of focus we have been talking about. In leadership, to actually contribute in ways that are lasting and sustaining, *presence* must take precedence over *position*.

Authentic leading involves compassionately and courageously creating environments that inspire and guide others to be all they can be. Great leading involves caring for people, not manipulating them. Ray Taillefer communicated this clearly when he talked about his commitment to build his company based on growing *people*. "I try not to focus on the sins in people or concentrate on their weaknesses. I prefer to see their *talents* and their *potential*... If measured, my success would be in terms of our people and how they have grown."

As a founder of a family ranching operation, Don Campbell spoke of his commitment to building a strong future by having strong successors in his family business. "That is vital. My goal is to create an opportunity for young people to grow, to develop their talents, improve their skills, and to hopefully become more successful than I am." Don defined leadership as "letting people grow." The commitment to developing people has been described well by Bev Suek:

> Leadership is about developing our power from within. I think what's often forgotten is that internal power is required to be a good leader. It can't be based on *having* power over other people. It has to be about strengthening how we feel about ourselves more than anything. That's number one. One of my goals is to develop inner power in the people who work for me so that they feel good about themselves, so that they end up feeling stronger and more important.

> Right now, as I speak, I'm contemplating whether I've accomplished that or not. Our workplace is really nice. We're very cooperative. We recognize employees' talents. We let them know they have control. Of course there are parameters, but we all have control over the work that we do. Most of the people here who are man-

agers and work directly with me have done that. They feel good about themselves. We don't have a formula or "steps" program. It's about believing in people and learning as we go.

Leaders we have interviewed, worked with and learned from over the years have a visible transforming impact on their people. It is real. It comes from the depths of their being. We could sense their presence in every interview. Even though they could not always articulate this sense of presence, we knew they had power from an internal presence. Perhaps the only real legacy you will leave is the imprint you make on the lives of the people you impact.

Finally, Bob Richardson, a real estate broker and consultant, perhaps best summarizes the difference between leading and leadership:

> ... I would say that 10% of the people run the world. They don't run the world because the world anointed them to do it. They run the world because they thought they were valuable human beings and had something to say and that they had a right to stand up and say, "This is how I want my world to be." I also think that I have the right to say, "This is how I want my world to be. And I want my world to be a progressive, loving place.

CHAPTER 3

———— ✻ ————

Breaking Away —
Connecting To Your
Authentic Self

We shall not cease from exploration
And the end of all our exploring
Will be to arrive where we started
And know the place for the first time.
—T. S. Eliot

* * * *

Michelangelo was once asked how he carved such magnificent works as *David* and the *Pietà*, works with such beauty and divinity, from a slab of marble. He reportedly replied, "I didn't do anything. God put the *Pietà* and *David* in the marble. They were already there. I only had to carve away the parts that kept you from seeing them... I saw an angel in the stone and carved to set it free."

83

AUTHENTICITY IS INNATE

Like *David* and the *Pietà* or a magnificent angel within a slab of marble, an authentic self is already within each of us. We come into the world psychologically and spiritually intact — it is the deepest nature of our being, our spiritual birthright.

Lessons from Infants and Children

When spending time with a newborn infant, we see the presence of authenticity in its purest form. Newborns instinctively ask for what they want even when adults may not understand their demands. Infants eat when hungry, sleep when tired, and cry when uncomfortable. Infants have no room for apology, inadequacy, or self-degradation, nor do they have motives for malice or manipulation. If we seek authenticity in life, infants are exceptional teachers.

Many parents — especially parents with more than one child — are keenly aware that each child is born with a distinct, unique authentic essence. For example, David's eldest daughter, Mellissa, has a "creative" essence, and expresses it through her pottery and artistic creations. If she is not expressing some sort of creativity, she will become disheartened and despondent. His second daughter, Hayley, on the other hand, is very spirited, continually pushing the boundaries of new frontiers and adventures, while Chandra is more intuitive and has a gentle, sensitive soul. Each of these children — like each one of us — is born with a distinct, unique authentic essence.

Challenges to the Soul

The soul is what we define as the essence of "who one is" at birth, that essential nature that lies below the surface of roles, titles, achievements, failures — all of the things that people use to define "who I am" during the course of human experience. Born "authentic," as infants we enter the world as "beings of light," but we abandon this light to satisfy the demands of well-meaning caretakers, families, and our surrounding culture, and in the process, we abandon our "selves." Societies operate through an establishment of roles — and we abandon ourselves to these roles in an effort to be a part of a society. Often, this happens very early in life. An authentic journey is, like Michelangelo's sculpting, an earnest, painstaking process of carving away the "marble" that is keeping us from seeing what is actually inside ourselves and bringing that unique, inner core out into the world.

Our premise is that this authentic self — the soul — is undoubtedly influenced by genetics and environment, but the soul has a powerful life-force, destined to be lived, beyond either genetics or environment. James Hillman[1] speaks to the power of the authentic self and challenges us to view the possibility of the soul with new thinking:

> … Today's main paradigm for understanding a human life, the interplay of genetics and environment, omits something essential — the particularity you feel to be you. By accepting the idea that I am the effect of a subtle buffeting between hereditary and social forces, I reduce myself to a result. The more my life is accounted for by what already occurred in my chromosomes, by what my parents did or didn't do, and by my early years now long past, the more my biography is the story of a victim. I am living a plot written by my genetic code, ancestral heredity, traumatic experiences, parental impact, and societal accidents… If any fantasy holds our contemporary civilization in an unyielding grip, it is that we are our parents' children and that the primary instrument of our fate is the behavior — and chromosomes — of our mothers and fathers.

An old Gnostic tradition says one does not *invent* things, one merely *remembers* things. This tradition is similar to an authentic journey. You don't *invent* or even *discover* authenticity; you actually only *remember* what is already there. The essence of who you are, of what you were when you were born, and of who you have always been — the *essential* authentic self (we call this the *soul*) — is what reconnects you to the universe from which you originated.

George McFaul summed it up well when asked how he thought a person becomes authentic. He shook his head and responded reflectively, "I think that's the wrong question. We're all *born* authentic. The question isn't how do you get to be authentic, but rather how do you *lose* your sense of authenticity in the first place?"

Ian West has a small altar to remind him, and the people he works with, of the authentic, spontaneous contribution of everyone in his organization. On the left-hand side of a slab of wood is a block of marble. On the right-hand side is Up-tai, the laughing Taoist monk. In the center is a clock that represents time. The altar is a visual reminder to this man that his task, throughout time, is to intentionally chip away at the ignorance that conceals the genius inside, which, when revealed, is a lighthearted perfected being.

AUTHENTICITY AND THE THREE SELVES

Now I become myself.
It's taken time, many years and places.
I have been dissolved and shaken,
Worn other people's faces...
—Mary Carton

Authentic leadership is about people who are dedicated to understanding their own uniqueness and hidden talents, people who have the courage to be that authentic person, and people who then inspire, support, and encourage other people on their journeys to find and express *their* voices. In a sense, the work of authentic leaders is to inspire and support other people on a "sculpting" journey. Yet, considering the strength of the human soul, how is the sense of authenticity lost in the first place? How is it that we lose contact with the authentic selves that we are born with? How do we stray so far from our authentic selves?

The Model Self

Although we are born "authentic," the soul instinctively knows that full authentic potential cannot be realized by remaining in a newborn state of beauty, awe, helplessness, and naiveté. We must experience a broad spectrum of encounters. As children, dependent upon our surroundings, the authentic self from birth encounters the *model* self or the expectations of the myriad of cultures surrounding us — families, friends, schools, communities, churches, and eventually workplaces. They tell us, "This is how you *should* be; this is what we deem to be *acceptable*." The message is clear: "If you want acceptance and recognition, this is what you should model." Therefore, the model self is what our environments — either consciously or unconsciously — deem to be acceptable within a particular culture.

Some cultures offer support and encouragement for the authentic self, while others are intolerant of any expression of uniqueness and push hard to change us. Either way, the cultures that we live in and their expectations or us (whether they undermine or support authentic growth), are *necessary* for instruction.

The Constructed Self

Surviving within our various surrounding cultures necessitates development of a *constructed* self — a self that we build in response to these cultures. If a particular environment does not mirror our authentic self, we tend to build a constructed self that fits the environment in an effort to meet our needs. As we align ourselves with the terms, conditions, and pressures of a culture, we lose contact with our own authentic self.

We then begin to identify with a model self by constructing a self that fits a particular culture rather than alignment with our authentic self. Some people call this constructed self a *false* self. Yet, this self is not false — in fact, it is very real. It is what we know ourselves to be, but it may not be very connected with our true authentic self.

As we move through the variety of cultures that surround us with this constructed self, we begin to move in directions that disconnect us from a sense of "oneness" with everything and everyone and the relationship with the "divinity" that is present at the beginning of life. Kate Harling describes it well:

> I think we come into the world with a certain essence of what we have inherited from our family lineage and culture and with a unique presence — an *authentic* self. And we have an instinctual urge to interact within our environment to get our needs met.
>
> As we go through life, from the moment we draw our first breath, we put parts of ourselves that are not mirrored by our environment or that don't work in our environment in a "black bag" that we carry behind us. And when we get to be adults, we have to spend the rest of our lives getting those parts out of the black bag.

Jim talks about the dangers of living under the cloud of cultural pressures.

> My father was a finishing carpenter, a true craftsman. Understandably, one of his most significant core values

was pride. Shortly after purchasing our first family home in Winnipeg, and mortgaging it to the hilt, he was laid off.

This dealt a crushing blow to his sense of pride. He had been raised in Russia where culture demanded that men be good providers and always be strong, so he suffered immensely as he tried to find new work, judging himself to be less than adequate in living up to expectations of the "model self."

I suspect he was in great pain because showing fear and vulnerability would have been perceived by him and others as being a sign of serious weakness. Thus, he was alone. No longer able to live with his perception of himself as a total failure as a husband and father, he chose to end his pain by ending his life — the only option he thought he had.

I am convinced that if he had received the permission, compassion, and understanding he needed to express how he felt authentically, he would have seen other options, and the outcome would have been different. The truth is that he was a tender, kind, gentle, and loving husband and father. He was merely between jobs! His perceptions were all wrong, but cultural pressures were extremely powerful.

Without question, genetics and family are important factors, especially during our early, formative years. Even in an environment that supports our authentic self, we sometimes construct a self that follows a path that is beyond genetic or environmental forces. We all know of people who make choices that take them away from the authentic self that a particular environment is attempting to nurture. Ask any loving, available, encouraging parent with high ideals who has lost a child to an addiction, a lack of focus or initiative, or even to suicide. Conversely, children who grow up in disheveled households, with seemingly little support or affirmation, often find ways to be creative contributors. It's a matter of destiny and it's a matter of choice.

Now consider Dave's story.

> For the most part, I grew up in a home that wholeheart-edly supported my authentic desires (which, as a preschooler, were for explicit love and nurturing) by giv-ing me permission to fill my room with dolls. Then in grade one (the school culture), I took all my dolls to class for show-and-tell. In that moment of humiliation and betrayal I experienced at school that day, I choose to box up my dolls — along with my authentic self — and to construct a self that lasted for many years. This self had a strong exterior, but it was far distant from my authen-tic self.

> Today, I believe that constructing a self that was separate from who I was caused me to spend much of my youth as an inarticulate, depressed teenager. But I also know that I could not do what I am doing today without this experience.

Seeking an Authentic Self

When interviewing people for this book, we were fascinated to learn about the different paths taken by people seeking to discover their authentic selves by interacting with the culture. Our first example is from Ben Wong's story. Ben told about growing up as a minority (Chinese) in a white society:

I had the advantage of being marginalized very early and very young. It gave me an opportunity to look inside myself, and I became introspective early in life. I realized I could never become one of "them." I couldn't be a blond-haired football player hero. I couldn't be the sex idol that many of my school colleagues wanted to be. All I could do was to succeed at school. So this was my advantage.

I felt rejection very early, when I was 6 or 7 years old and kids chased me home from school, calling me a "Chink." All along, I always thought I was okay. I just didn't understand why other people didn't think I was.

Next is Jock McKeen's story. Jock's appreciation of authenticity is from an opposite situation:

I had lots of smiles, big beaming smiles, mostly from my parents and my grandmother. And their message was, "You're so wonderful." "You can become something really great!" So, in a sense, it was a bit "demonic" that I sort of forgot about my soul and got into a project of "What can I turn myself into." In some ways, my opinion of myself was false. On the surface, I thought I was great, but underneath, a type of self-hatred was functioning. Below the surface, I actually hated myself, which explained my inclination toward addictive behaviors. I think I was completely dependent on other people's opinions. I was really out of touch with my authentic being. My social connections at that time were based on my charisma rather than my authentic being. I didn't know my authentic being. In a way, inwardly, I was in despair!

Jock also says that, through his relationships, especially with Ben Wong, he began to realize that his own opinion of himself had more value than other people's opinions. He describes the feeling of being authentic: "I feel calm inside. It is in contrast to that uncertain, exciting, but ever-ready-to-change unpredictability that I feel when I'm in a power structure."

RECONCILING THE THREE SELVES — THE AUTHENTIC JOURNEY

Lessons from Childhood

In an interview, Don Calveley described a defining moment in his authentic journey — a moment when it became clear that he needed to live by fundamental principles and have a mission in life to begin constructing a self more in alignment with his authentic self:

> I grew up hunting and fishing every weekend with my father. We usually hunted for pheasants, grouse, and duck. I recall doing that until about age 15. One day, on the first day of the new duck-hunting season, we were up in the highlands to "scare a lake." This is when one person goes to the opposite side of the lake to scare the ducks and send them up in the air in the direction of the other people who are waiting with their shotguns in hand.
>
> On this particular morning, it was my turn to scare the ducks. But when I arrived at the other side of the lake, I came across an entire family of ducks — actually numerous families of ducks — waddling around and playing with their young. The sun was shining. It was an idyllic moment of natural beauty. I could not scare those ducks.

It was the first time in my life that the thought had registered with me that "I have a mind and I have a choice and I don't want to do this." Even with the ribbing of all the other hunters on the other side of the lake, I wouldn't do it.

At that time, I was a young, bravado-type of youngster who rode motorcycles and did all sorts of things to show off. But this was a moment of reflection and a moment of a choice — and I had made my choice. I put down my gun that day, and I have never hunted again. It's just one of those things that a person makes a decision about.

For me, it was sort of a spiritual decision. I saw the beauty of the moment, and I chose not to disturb it. It was one of those moments that resonate throughout life. And it was my introduction to recognizing that there's a balance in life and there are choices in life. That day I chose to live a life that includes people and animals and nature and a lot of other things. I think that day was the first stepping stone for me — just realizing that I was my own person and that I didn't need to follow along with a herd or public opinion…

Talk about a difficult situation — to actually make that kind of a choice. That day I was with my peers and comrades, with my father, and with my best friend and my best friend's father.

Then we asked, "And how did your father respond?" Don replied:

It was interesting, actually. When I came back to the group, a couple of jokes were made, but I just said, "I'm over it, guys. I'm not interested in hunting anymore. Clay pigeons, skeet shooting, fine, that's no problem.

But that's a sport. These are animals and they're happy..." I don't have an issue with hunting per se if you're eating what you're hunting. I'm just choosing not to do it anymore.

My father was at an age and a time in his life when hunting was a way to stay connected to me. By us spending time together, he thought he was doing it for me because I was a teenager and he wanted us to have a close relationship. That was important to him. So we discussed it and he agreed with me. He thought my decision was fine.

As we track our lives through the tapestry of our experiences — in environments that support our authentic presence and in environments that reject it — we will discover a sense of calling, a destiny, or a "voice" that leads us toward finding our authentic gifts. Jerry Weinberg describes catching a glimpse of his authentic self by reflecting on an experience when he was 8 years old:

I was a smart kid. And everyone kept telling me I was smart. It occurred to me that if I were smart, I ought to be able to understand how to make things happen the way I wanted them to happen. What else could smart mean?

What I wanted was to be happy. But how could I convert smart into being happy? When I was 8 years old, I committed myself to that — to learning how to convert smart into happy. I see a lot of smart people who are using their brains to make themselves miserable — they don't see the connection between what they're doing and what they're getting. If you're not enjoying something while you're doing it, that's a warning that maybe you're doing something that's not harmonious or that's inconsistent within oneself.

Lessons from the Workplace

Another experience was related to us by Mary Martin who received a painful performance appraisal early in her career. Yet, this experience turned out to be pivotal in the work she now does in the organizational development field:

> In 1971, during my very first performance appraisal, I was told I was too "enthusiastic." I remember that because it was such a shock to hear. Of course, nobody explained what "too enthusiastic" meant, and at that stage of my career I didn't even know enough to ask. But I will always remember this experience and its impact on me. I'll never forget the pain of trying to live up to the expectations of a culture, but compromising my authentic self in the process. A resolve emerged from this experience that has led me to work "around" the traditional performance measurement systems used in most organizations.
>
> I now value authenticity because I recognize it has value in building a vibrant, engaged, productive culture. Something genuine and real exists within everyone. It's always within us. Honoring this authentic self in ourselves and in others forms a basis for respect, trust, and subsequently energy in an organization.

Although these stories illustrate some of the numerous responses to inauthentic cultures, often we can be immersed in a culture that is *supportive* of our authentic selves. Consider Jim's experience of constructing an authentic self in an authentically encouraging culture:

> Hewlett-Packard, where I worked for many years, had, at least at that time, a very strong, powerful culture that fostered authenticity. I believe this culture was one of the primary reasons that HP was many times ranked as one of the best companies to work for in North America. As an HP manager, I knew exactly what the company expected of me. The core values of the organization were published so all stakeholders — employees, customers, and shareholders — would have a clear understanding of what HP stood for. When I hired new team members, I would focus much of my attention on trying to determine if potential employees shared the HP values. If they did, the chances were that they would be far more committed and be longer-term employees who would enjoy working alongside other people who shared these same values and principles. In fact, Hewlett Packard told me to think of my leadership role as being a "harmonizer of values." In those days, we talked about the "HP Way," which was an unwritten, but clearly understood, code of conduct that all HP employees lived by in their daily dealings with customers and with their fellow employees. I think this strong cultural environment that had been created by the founders in the early days of their legendary partnership was one of the most critical factors in HP's long run of unprecedented growth and success.

A sign of an authentic culture is one that makes its expectations explicit. When an organization's values and guiding principles are clearly understood, published and promoted, they act as magnets to attract like-minded people. In a business culture, vision and goals are required, but the values and belief systems that we as individuals choose are at the core of promoting authenticity. As contributors in the field of leadership, we are committed to creating cultures in which authenticity is supported, acknowledged, and promoted.

How Do I Recognize Authenticity?

Authenticity does not have to look a certain way. The real strength of Jim's early years at HP was that the people at HP were *honest* and *explicit* about what they stood for. This type of environment is authenticity at its finest — people know where they stand and have the freedom to choose accordingly.

When we are exposed to different cultures, authenticity is deciding how much of our authentic selves we are willing to give up. Sometimes, because we want to fit into a certain culture, we begin to give up parts of ourselves.

In our formative years, it is easy to surrender to the culture in which we live, and then remain enslaved to these patterns for years. A classic example of this is an overachiever. Overachievers often began as youngsters who learned at an early age that they must *prove* themselves in order to be valued by their parents or care-givers. If these individuals do not become conscious of this outdated belief system, they may become so far removed from the voice of their own authentic selves that they spend entire lifetimes relentlessly achieving and seeking approval outside themselves. An overachiever is an example of one end of a "constructed" continuum, in which the self can be totally lost in cultural expectations.

The other end of the constructed continuum spectrum is to completely withdraw from a culture. For example, perhaps you detest or resent a culture. You might say something like, "I don't want any part of the establishment. I'll do my thing, and you can do your thing." Although this stance could certainly be an authentic response in certain circumstances, if *all* cultures were consolidated into one sweeping generalization, the effect of this stance would be total refusal to participate in society. Without doubt, this choice will result in a loss of potential for the fulfilling, authentic growth that results from reflective interaction with the culture. Remember: An authentic self has the power of choice.

Usually, most people are somewhere in the middle, giving up different parts of themselves during certain phases of life and reclaiming some parts during other phases. We need interaction with the model self. Our purpose is to interact with our culture, to push back at it or flow with it, and in the process to discover more fully what fits and what does not. An authentic journey can never be completed in isolation. A significant part of growth and evolution of the soul is *choosing* the values — and cultures — that best represent the authentic self. It is less about giving up, and more about *matching* up.

Applying the Model of the Three Selves

As leaders, our goal is to inspire communities that are committed to providing a place where it is okay to be "who you are," without expectations that we must fit into a certain mold. Obviously, at an organizational level, expectations are required, but it is essential to make these expectations explicit so that everyone is aware of the choices available for aligning these expectations with their authentic selves.

Our belief is that we *can* step back and begin reclaiming our authenticity and not completely lose ourselves in a culture or relationship. We learn from cultures and relationships. Which ones are supportive? Which ones erode the spirit? Which ones have positive lessons? Which ones are contributing to the loss of oneself? These questions are not intended to imply a form of judgment, but are simply an invitation to remain conscious, which will enable choices of more appropriate responses that support an authentic journey.

The model of the three selves can raise our awareness of just how immersed we have become in the culture or cultures in which we live and work.

We are always in a state of evolving from what a culture expects of us to what is yearned for by our authentic selves. A journey to regain authenticity begins with a feeling of incongruity between what the world offers and the deeper yearnings of the soul. Perhaps it is a sense of estrangement about how we are living life and how life wants to be lived within us. Perhaps we have constructed a highly functioning model self, which has a CEO role, with a Ph.D. and tenure in a current position. There is a BMW in the driveway of a very nice house. Success is there in all the ways that our culture says is important, but in the middle of the night, we feel empty. This success looks like gold, feels like gold, and even smells like gold, but it can become a trap if we over-identify with this model self and its accompanying rules and beliefs.

The goal of a path toward reconciling the three selves is not to discard a constructed self, but to become more porous so the light of an essential self can shine through. As we begin to reconnect with our own authentic self, we become more real and our masks loosen their attachment. We become more interested in taking our masks off, perhaps interchanging or modifying them, rather than identifying too tightly with one particular mask.

Instead of discarding our constructed selves, an awareness of the differences between our constructed, model, and authentic selves enables us to make more conscious choices in life. By being aware of the differences, we approach life situations with better clarity about when to be our constructed self and when we should be more authentic. Making choices more explicitly leads to greater authenticity — for us and in our impact on other people.

Being aware of the model of the three selves in his life today is important to Jim. He relates it in another story.

When I was younger and still focused on building my business career, I naturally spent significant amounts of time in cultural environments that viewed materialistic success as a primary measure for acceptance. I have nothing against this type of environment, but financial success is not the only thing that is important to me.

Over time, I was increasingly turning away from these "more is better" materialistic communities and searching for places where I would be accepted for who I was, with all my warts and insecurities. I found it increasingly difficult to find close friends who would support and encourage me on my authentic journey. Now, when I can't find these communities, I'm motivated to try and create them.

Life is so much more invigorating when I can just be "who I am" and you can be "you."

Jim concludes with,

When I am stressed or out-of-sorts, it is usually because I am looking externally instead of internally for approval.

An authentic journey is investigating and searching for the true nature of our identity, understanding how we stray so far from ourselves in the first place, getting back on the path that is in alignment with who we really are, and then bringing that authentic essence to our work in leadership.

AUTHENTIC LIVING, ALIGNMENT, AND STRESS

Burnout comes not from hard work but from heartache.
—Rabbi Ira Eisenstein

Alignment in the Workplace

The essence of an authentic journey is to continue the quest to achieve alignment of the desires of one's soul and the demands of society and at the same time to build a constructed self that aligns the two forces of desires and demands. Aligning these forces is a key to achieving inner peace, just as surely as separating these forces results in stress.

This quest is not just a spiritual one. It also has practical application in the business environment. The more we identify with things that are not true to who we really are, the less able we will be to communicate, coordinate actions, contribute, and learn effectively. Finding out who we really are and aligning our values, unique talents, passions, and higher purpose with the needs of the organizations in which we work will become a fundamental business imperative. This alignment between our souls and our workplaces, which is where we find and express our gifts in the service of others, is at the root of a productive, life-enhancing, and sustainable organization.

Alignment in an organization begins with personal internal alignment. Take a look at the dynamics of personal internal alignment with some practical examples. For example, if you are an entrepreneur trying to make it in the marketplace, you will likely be expected to adhere to a certain dress code. If you go into a bank to ask for a $1 million loan to start a high-tech business venture wearing a T-shirt and jeans, your credibility would, in all likelihood, be significantly reduced. In this example, you are not being inauthentic by wearing a suit and tie. Putting on a suit and tie is not a moral or ethical issue, even if your "authentic self" would prefer not to wear one. Wearing a suit is simply the most appropriate in these circumstances.

Now consider another example. In an earlier career as a sales representative before coming to Hewlett Packard, Jim once received a substantial order that had a large commission. The customer had a very specific deadline for a new computer system. The customer said, "If you can't meet this deadline, please let me know because I will then have to go with another company." Management at the factory Jim used said that they could meet the target, but within a month of the deadline, they called to say that their commitment could not be met.

Jim's immediate response was, "I've got to tell the customer right away that circumstances have changed and I will be unable to meet their deadline because I made a promise to them that I would do that." His boss responded, "No, we're going to lose that order if we do. The customer was clear. They'll go somewhere else. They'll cancel the order."

The implied demand was, "Just go ahead and lie," assuming that if they waited long enough, it would be too late for the customer to order the computer system from another company. In the culture of that company, it was okay to lie to customers — clearly an ethical and moral issue. Jim immediately made a decision to not compromise his principles and left that company. If you don't have the courage to stand tall on principles that matter, your authentic self will be eroded and in the process, so will your self-respect and confidence.

Our hope is that thinking about decisions from this approach will result in your making values-based decisions consciously, being able to ask honestly, "Is it okay, in this particular circumstance, for me to be inauthentic?" You can have more clarity and become more courageous about issues that are important to you because you will begin to recognize the issues that are open for compromise and the ones that are not. By using this process, you will grow as an individual. Understanding and discerning the differences between the authentic self, the constructed self, and the cultural expectations of the model self brings clarity and a framework for decision-making. It is a practical tool and a process to make life simpler and more meaningful.

Consciously or unconsciously, everyone is constructing a life that is somewhere between the authentic self and the model self. The goal is to do this and remain committed to both clarity and consciousness — clarity by continually seeking your authentic voice and consciousness by tuning-in when you are off balance. Stress is a barometer that indicates when clarity and consciousness are out of balance.

Integrating the Three Selves in a Culture

When continually working to integrate the three selves, watch for two distinct types of stress — conscious and unconscious stress. *Conscious* — or *authentic* — stress results from having a commitment to be authentic in an inauthentic culture. Conscious stress will be the natural result of choosing to do the best we can to be authentic in inauthentic cultures. Without doubt, a culture can contribute to movement away from our true selves by asking us to act in certain ways that might not be congruent with "who we are." *Unconscious* — or *inauthentic* — stress is far more destructive. It contributes to disease, bitterness, and despondency in one's life. Unconscious stress is a result of losing ourselves in a culture — succumbing to a culture that we live or work in because of insecurity or having a lack of clarity about our own authentic self. Let's look at both types of stress in more detail.

Conscious Stress

At times in our life we find ourselves trying to be authentic in an inauthentic culture. For example, perhaps you work in an organization that considers leaving work at 5:00 p.m. to be negative or to indicate a lack of commitment, where employees who work 12-14-hour days and come in on weekends are rewarded; or perhaps a company does not acknowledge that its levels of bureaucracy obstruct creative thinking and innovation; or perhaps an organization only rewards increasing financial results. You may feel that for you, these types of environments are not good to be in. They are not "who you are," but you continue to work there because you need this particular job at this time in your life.

Negotiating and deciding to stay and work hard for only 8 to 10 hours a day in this type of environment will be stressful. In all likelihood, there will be some peer pressure or you will experience additional stress from missing out on promotional opportunities because you are not willing to make compromises, but you have made a conscious decision to stay. Conscious stress can be challenging during the workday, but you will have a sense of self-respect at the end of the day, knowing that you are living life in alignment with your values.

Another example of conscious stress is deciding to stay in a marriage or a significant relationship to maintain stability for the children or because, after careful consideration, it is just not right to leave. You might make a conscious choice to stay in a relationship, knowing that there will be disparity between this culture and your own authentic self, but that you will strive to be true to your own self as best you can within that relationship. It will be stressful, but you are remaining conscious. In times like these, you have the option to reach out to other people who can support you authentically and strengthen your participation in a particular relationship.

The beauty of this model is that we remind ourselves that we can be authentic when faced with inauthentic environments. Important: We will always be somewhere between our culture and our own authentic self. There is no perfect map or perfect life. But we can decide, "I am in this culture, but I will not lie, cheat, or steal. I know where the line is drawn that I will not cross... I will not submit to abuse or compromise my core values... I will not buy into the notion that I am only as good as my last quarter... I may have to wear a tie and show up in ways that are not my preference, but by doing so I am not compromising my value system or my integrity."

Managing Conscious Stress

Although conscious stress is experienced regularly by those who work in non-authentic cultures, using the principles of authenticity can make this stress more manageable. It is the non-destructive stress from decisions made with clarity and self-awareness which either work or do not. The antidote to this type of conscious stress is to courageously do our best and do so as authentically as possible. We do not try to provide leadership to people who do not share our values and goals or want the same things we do. Our leadership is not to convince people to have different values — that would be proselytizing and not the authentic type of leadership we are seeking. By remaining true to our own authentic selves and values, we generally attract people who are drawn to these same values. If people are not attracted to our leadership and what it has to offer, simply move on. This type of conscious stress is, indeed, challenging at times, but it becomes less so with clarity, practice and persistence.

The Role of Misalignment in Conscious Stress

Although alignment is a source of serenity, misalignment with the authentic self is the greatest source of destructive stress in modern civilization. It is not overwork that is hurting us as a society — it is *misalignment* with our soul's desires.

John Charette, a 32-year career public servant, expressed well the meaning of authenticity with a clear example of "conscious stress" and what it means to live life in alignment with one's values:

> In simplest terms, authenticity is "what you see is what you get." I may have a role in what I'm doing, but what's underneath that role is still authentic. I might face challenges and stress in my job when I have many roles in my life and in my day-to-day interacting with others, but at the bottom of it all, authenticity is knowing who I am, what I stand for, and what the values are that drive me and guide my behavior in a way that's aligned with those values.

Unconscious Stress

Unconscious stress is an entirely different situation. It is a result of being *inauthentic*, especially when we are unaware of doing so. It emerges when we have a lack of commitment to clarity and consciousness. Unconscious stress results from compromising ourselves by living in a culture that we allow to shut down our authentic expression and capacity. The stress of living inauthentically contributes to illness, bitterness, and despondency. People who have succumbed to unconscious stress are easy to spot. Bureaucracies are full of unhappy, stressed-out, toxic individuals who are merely getting by in the workplace or "doing time" in their jobs — as if they were in prison or counting the days to retirement.

Another type of unconscious stress is less obvious and more subtle — the stress of keeping up with societal expectations. Everyone is susceptible to the stress of trying to keep up with cultural expectations.

Think of the constructed self as another view of our self-image, which ultimately determines what "is" or "is not" possible for us. If we (usually unconsciously) want to live up to the cultural expectations for acceptance, but we do not measure up (e.g., we own the smallest house on the street or drive the least-expensive car in the neighborhood), then our self-image suffers. We could be doing very well by some people's standards, yet there are always expectations from our cultural environment that we cannot meet. Someone always has a bigger house, a more expensive car, or lives in a nicer neighborhood. If we define ourselves according to the opinions or approval of other people, and strive harder and harder to be part of a culture, we move farther and farther away from our core values and selves. How many times have we seen ourselves or others assume larger mortgages or increase personal debt levels as a result of greed, fear, or a need for approval from other people? Always remember: As soon as we catch up with the Joneses, inevitably they will refinance!

Some Final Thoughts

Different segments of the cultures we live in will compete for our attention by making opposing demands. These demands pull us in so many directions that we can lose contact with the inner voice of intuition that leads us to authenticity. Once again, the key is to stay awake, seek clarity of the yearning of the authentic self, and stand firm on the courage of our convictions. In the process, anxiety and stress levels will be replaced with some degree of serenity and inner peace.

Tim Dutton talked to us about his experience of being pulled in many directions, and the importance of maintaining a sense of self. It is an experience that is common in our world today:

> I think that all of us want to please, but the tension comes from not losing "me" in the process. I've got two

81-year-old parents. Lord knows I want to please them, but the challenge is how to figure out the way to be of service to them while maintaining my own identity in life. I think it's not so much about abandoning the desire we all have to please, but more about figuring out how to deal with the tension that arises.

ENDNOTE

1. James Hillman. 1996. *The Soul's Code: In Search of Character and Calling*, pp. 6, 63. New York: Random House.

CHAPTER 4

Recognizing Authentic
Action In Leadership —
Eight Qualities Of
Presence

*Four thousand volumes of metaphysics
will not teach us what the soul is.*
—Voltaire

* * * *

NOW, HAVING A BASIC UNDERSTANDING of the principles of authentic action and of some of the root causes why leaders stray so far from authenticity in the first place, we will turn our focus more precisely to the "look and feel" of a path of authenticity. But first, think about two questions: How do I recognize when I am leading authentically? And what impact do I have on other people when I am authentic?

THE EIGHT QUALITIES OF AUTHENTIC PRESENCE

To answer these questions, we will examine eight qualities of authentic action: clarity, courage, integrity, service, trust, humility, compassion, and vulnerability. These qualities describe characteristics that we have observed in authentic people. Keep in mind five important points about these eight qualities:

- Compare the list to the actions of the authentic people in your life. Based on your reflections, catch these people being authentic. Remember: That which you focus on is what will grow. The best way to grow authenticity is to pay attention to it. You may also find as you read and reflect on these qualities that some areas need your attention and focus. Make a gentle commitment to yourself to take action in the areas you want to strengthen, beginning with *yourself*.

- Our list is not exhaustive. Without a doubt, you could make a list of qualities from your observations. We encourage you to do that. Make these qualities your own. Take what fits, and leave the rest, but keep an open mind.

- Authenticity is not nearly as linear or delineated as the qualities indicate. Each of the eight qualities depends on all the other qualities to have lasting impact and sustained presence. For example, service without clarity could result in burnout. Humility without integrity could result in frailty. Courage without compassion might end up as brutality. So as you read about these qualities, try to see them not as separate entities, but rather as a part of an indivisible whole that describes authentic leadership in action.

- Describing authenticity is like describing the soul — it cannot be done by *words*, but by *action*. Our description of authenticity is far from actual authenticity itself. We attempt to describe authentic actions through theory and stories, but they cannot replace the *experience* of being in the presence of authenticity. Our stories and theories are to inspire and guide you to *live* more authentically.

• Reading and reflection on the eight qualities calls for new actions, but remember: authenticity does not demand any degree of perfection. In fact, it is the antithesis of appearing to be perfect. Authenticity is realness, honesty, and humanness. It is not pretending to be closer to being authentic than we actually are. Authenticity is recognizing that we have the human spiritual quality of free will, we are truthful with ourselves and others, and that we act accordingly.

By outlining the eight qualities, our intention is to paint a mental picture from our perspective of the path of authentic leadership so that you will recognize authentic leadership actions in yourself and others. The qualities of authentic presence are in each of us, especially in people who are committed to making an authentic difference in the lives of others. Yet, authentic leadership is not mastering these traits as much as carefully examining our responses to them in our environment. While reading about the qualities of authenticity, take time to carefully consider the consequences of living in disharmony with them vs. the characteristics and the rewards of living in accord with them.

Our thoughts in this chapter are from experiences of trying to live in alignment with these qualities and observing others striving to do the same. These experiences have expanded our perceptions and have provided leverage to change the course of our work and our lives. We trust they will do the same for you.

CHARACTERISTICS OF AUTHENTIC RESPONSES

We use several observations and general characteristics to describe authentic responses. Authentic people:

- Recognize that they are spiritual beings with a free will and accept that the results they produce in their lives are a direct reflection of the choices they make

- Hold themselves accountable for the choices they make and for living in alignment with their highest principles

- Respect the choices that other people make

- Choose their own set of beliefs about life, knowing that this empowers them to create their own results

- Strive to live in the present with passion, faith, courage and compassion

- Possess unwavering personal integrity by following a steadfast set of sustaining principles in living life, both in the limelight and in private

- Relentlessly strive to keep their word to themselves and with other people

- Make a commitment to self-discovery and lifelong learning from other people and from life's setbacks, knowing that every experience is a learning opportunity, every obstacle is a potential lesson, and every frustration an opportunity to make a shift to choosing *curiosity*

Before exploring the eight specific qualities of authentic action, reflect on how some of the people we interviewed describe authentic actions in a wide range of leadership settings.

Caroline Missal: "I think that when you're willing to admit that you don't have all the answers, the result is more honest conversations with staff and teachers because they don't feel that they have to have all the answers either."

Mary Michailides: "It's asking, 'How do I value the relationships that I work with daily?'"

Judy Walton: "The interesting thing about being open and not having all the answers is that it's something that helps create the answers."

Kate Harling: "It's about trusting yourself and trusting the unknown and trusting that there's something guiding you in life that is much greater than you'll ever understand. It's internal and you can sense that it's there. I completely relate that to leadership — because I have to be 'set' with myself when I'm in a leadership position."

Dale Kelly: "You can't be a very effective or authentic leader without having a strong self-awareness and people in your life who know that you want to be challenged about what you're doing and how you're doing it."

Rob Reid: "This one teacher I had thought 'outside the box.' He made all of us think that way, too. It wasn't just reading pages and spitting it all back in order. We went against the grain when it came to the curriculum that year, and it was a year that none of us have ever recovered from. We were doing things that made a difference. I was greatly influenced because this teacher was genuinely interested in each person and their development as opposed to what grade they'd get."

Don Campbell: "You need to accept people as they really are, realizing that they're all different. And that each one has a different talent, a different gift, and a different way of seeing things. I have learned just to focus on what is best for our family or what is best for our business, not that it is my idea because I am the dad, owner, or boss. And once I did that, I became more humble and got better answers because it didn't matter whose idea it was. If it gets better, why not take it?"

Gerry Zimmerman: "Look around and analyze some of the people you see every day — the 'jelly bean leader'; the 'it's not ever my fault leader'; and the 'I'm the toughest guy in the world leader.' Now, would you rather work for them or would you rather work for someone who shows their feelings and who treats you like a human being? My philosophy is that the janitor is just as important as the front-line firefighters. He has a job to do and so do they. The day that I start valuing one person above another, I think that's the day I start going backward. I think that if there's one thing a leader needs to know, it's that everyone has to be valued."

Mary Martin: "I don't know if I can fully describe those moments when I am in that 'authentic place,' but I know it's the real thing. It's kind of like the genuine me, the real me. There are a couple of things that happen. It feels easy because I'm at ease, as opposed to being anxious or concerned about how I'll be perceived or worried about all the other things that my ego attaches to. When I'm in the moment, I'm in the 'flow.' It's effortless. I feel clear, centered, and grounded. It feels 'right.' The impact is usually in service and somehow there's something happening that just works. I know that when I'm not in those 'moments,' it's generally because I'm working too hard. That's the difference for me."

Now let's turn our attention to the eight specific qualities of authentic action: clarity, courage, integrity, service, trust, humility, compassion, and vulnerability.

CLARITY — THE POWER OF FOCUS

Leadership is going where nobody else has gone.
—**Bob Galvin**, Son of the founder of Motorola

Few people who make contributions and live full lives in our society are immune from enormous daily environmental pressure. On some days, life seems to be nothing more than a messy trail of uncompleted to-do lists and unmet responses to a demanding world. The thoughts of unanswered e-mails, missed opportunities, unvisited friends, abandoned talents, and neglected commitments haunt our tranquil moments when we stop and reflect upon our lives.

Reflect for a moment on this poem[1] and the questions it subsequently raises:

What in your life is calling you?

When all the noise is silenced,

the meetings adjourned,

the lists laid aside,

and the wild iris blooms by itself

in the dark forest,

what still pulls on your soul?

In the silence between your heartbeats

hides a summons.

Do you hear it?

Name it, if you must,

or leave it forever nameless,

but why pretend it is not there.

— Thermal Collective

Authentic leaders are on a path to seek clarity. They are compelled to a lifelong journey of knowing their voice, their soul, and their purpose — and then acting on this awareness as they inspire and support other people to do the same. Consider these questions:

- How do I find my voice amidst all the demands of the culture I live in?

- How do I lose track and wander away from myself?

- How does knowing my voice impact my life and the lives of people I serve?
- What is the compelling vision that I am committed to engage and enlist others in?

What Is Clarity?

Clarity concerns letting our own voice come through. Our voice is always there, but the more aligned we are with what a culture wants from us, the more our voice is buried. Yet, as we begin to make contact with and awaken to the inner voice that is in the "silence between your heartbeats," the more we will become aware of what we want life to look like. As we have more clarity about what we want life to be, greater clarity is acquired — clarity about accepting or rejecting situations and opportunities as they arise.

Challenges to Clarity and Focus

Being authentic is meeting the challenge of achieving clarity and keeping focused on important things. We live in a culture that seems to continually sidetrack us with justifications, rationalizations, and urgings to turn a blind eye to our values under the guise that doing so is a requirement of success or getting ahead or achieving approval from other people. At times, it is a struggle when we are on the "out" side of culture. Clarity gives us permission to listen to and trust ourselves.

As we write this book, teachers are striking in our province. Just last evening we were in a conversation with a principal who was right in the middle of the chaos. Yet, by reflecting on her authentic journey and on a deep desire to find her inner voice, she lifted her chin, saying, "I'm going to start listening and trust myself!" She continued, "The unions aren't right. The government isn't right. What's right is that we need to be in there educating our kids. If I didn't believe in myself and trust in my own voice, I might have caved in to what the union and the government are saying, but now I'll stand firm on what I truly believe."

This situation illustrates having clarity at its finest. Sometimes it is there. Many times it is not. Yet, authenticity requires "staying the course" by continuing to listen to the voice of the soul in the midst of the noise of the culture.

If we stop long enough to thoughtfully examine our lives, we will soon realize that the dilemma of making room for our ever-increasing demands is far more complicated than just not having enough time. It is actually a challenge to *make room* in our lives to listen carefully to the summons from within, trusting the voice that emerges, and then living in accord with our core values and principles.

The clarity to confidently know which things are most important is a result of having a deep and sustaining core sense of *inner* security. Authentic people are on a lifelong journey. They do not need to keep up with anyone or impress anyone. They do not need possessions to have a sense of worth. They neither need nor depend on the approval of others and, therefore, are able to say "no" more easily to urgent requests that are not in alignment with their values.

For these people, because their accomplishments are an *expression* of their authentic selves rather than a *definition* of their worth, they find balance amidst their achievements. Authentic people are *comfortable* with themselves. They do not depend on affirmation from their culture; this allows them a greater sense of acceptance, calmness, and clarity about priorities. Authentic people know that striving to satisfy the obsessive need for "more" that is prevalent in society produces only emptiness.

Finding Clarity

Finding an ever-increasing sense of clarity is unique for each person. There are no formulas or simple "10-step" processes to achieve relief from the struggle. Instead, there are only examples of people who strive to live with authentic clarity. Consider the example of Don Campbell.

Don Campbell is a rancher. He is a source of inspiration for many people because he lives in accord with his values. He is comfortable with himself, independent of his successes and failures. Don knows what is important and lives accordingly. Although we use Don as an example of clarity in expressing authentic actions, clarity can be expressed in several ways. For some, clarity is expressed by their core values. For others, clarity is articulated by a goal for a higher purpose or by a calling. About clarity, Don says:

> I manage my life and our ranch with three core areas at the forefront: how to care for our people, how to improve our land, and how to make a profit. Our *Quality of Life* statement[2] is a three-part goal from these areas. This statement focuses on *what* we want for our people, *how* we want to treat each other, *what* each of us values, and what is important to each of us and to all of us. It also addresses how we will produce and how hard we need to work to support that quality of life.
>
> Our statement also talks about our land and the ecosystem surrounding it — what it must look like, not only today, but tomorrow, so that in 150 years, people will be able to live in a viable agricultural nation. Having this statement clearly in our minds gives us a framework for leadership and decision-making. We base our lives and our work on a clear goal and regular monitoring to

ensure that we stay on track with the things that matter most to each of us.

I compare having my clear *Quality of Life* statement to the North Star. It's like a guidance system. If we say this is the way my life will be, and this is what success looks like to us as a team, then when something comes up, we can measure it. The question always in the forefront is, "Does this decision take us toward the goal?" If so, great. We'll do it. If a decision takes us away from our goal, why would we do it?

Using this approach, something we call a "holistic framework," gives us a way to sort through all the pressures to do this or that or do it this way or that way. If we didn't have this mechanism, we'd be driven by society, advertising, and trends. We have a decision-making process so that we don't sacrifice people or land or money. We have to balance all three.

Because everyone tends to do whatever they're good at or like best or what is easy or familiar, we could lose touch with the North Star and lose our balance. But holistic management helps us achieve real balance in life. Our quality of life is better, our profits are higher (even when in a crisis year), and our land is better land, which means this ranch will be more sustainable in the future.

Don's *Quality of Life* statement was developed by the entire family within the family business. The following is a part of the statement:

B-C Ranch strives to provide personal contentment through maintaining a fun, fulfilling, open, and honest environment for its people. It is a sanctuary for lifelong learning, personal growth, and individual endeavors. It provides opportunity for all family members to be directly or indirectly involved in the ranch. It is a tool to ensure a strong family bond. B-C team members share the values of being accountable, reliable, responsible, and respectful. We will continue to share our ideas with others in the community. We are striving for excellence by being the best that we can be in people, land, and finances.

As mentioned, with these intentions clearly stated, this statement is not only a North Star, a framework for decision-making. It has a clear intention of opening doors for quality to flow into the family and the business. When they are not living in accord with the agreements and commitments they have made, the statement gives each person the ability to say, "Just a minute, we're not being respectful. We're not being responsible. And we all agreed we would…"

Don does not have to hold himself to his principles alone. He has five other people who can come to him and ask, "Are you being accountable to what we said we were going to be and do?" He has a support and an accountability team that is already in place.

On a personal level, Don has nine principles that guide him; these form his personal creed:

1. My time and talents are gifts from God.

2. My conduct reflects my belief that God is always present.

3. I must render an account of time lost, talents wasted, and complacency.

4. God will never test me beyond my strength.

5. I am a good steward of my time, talents, and money.

6. I am a lifelong learner.

7. People are my first priority.

8. I freely share my time, talents, philosophy, and wisdom with those I meet.

9. Time flies — remember death.

Don has memorized these principles and repeats them every day, which helps him remember that no matter how much money he has or what he possesses; how much pain or suffering he has to endure; and no matter what opinion anyone has of him, his worth of himself will always be intact because he lives in accord with his core principles.

Now, consider this family story told by Jim that puts another spin on the meaning of clarity.

> My older sister Lorie has dedicated her life to the service of other people. Ever since my wife Joan met Lorie many years ago, she has always thought that Lorie "should be kinder to herself and not let other people take advantage of her giving nature." But after reading our description of the three selves, specifically about clarity, Joan says she has changed her mind: "Now I see that Lorie is quite content to be a giver — this is who she is. This is the authentic Lorie being true to herself."

An expectation of another person, like Joan's expectation that Lorie should be more "selfish," is an expectation from the *model self* and not in alignment with Lorie's authentic being. Joan now has greater clarity about this as well.

Clarity Is Powerful

Regardless of the process used to seek clarity, ending this section with some final thoughts about clarity and the power of focus is important. Authentic clarity is not an ambitious determination that propels us toward achievement at all costs. All of the authentic actions that we have witnessed have been in the pursuit of things that are more substantive and more sustainable than material success.

When viewed through the lenses of authenticity, clarity allows actions to take place using clear intentions and a commitment to make our environment a better place.

Authentic clarity is about cooperating and aligning with an all-encompassing force in the universe, which continually supports and guides us — no matter how this force is expressed or understood.

Some Concluding Questions

- What does clarity mean to me?
- What defines me?
- What is my source of security?
- How do I measure my worth — aside from roles, achievements, possessions, and reputation?
- How do I get off track from my voice and my values and lose touch with what matters most?
- How do I find clarity in life?
- How am I held accountable to stay on track?
- Who gives me support?
- If I were to write out a quality of life statement, what would it say?
- What core areas would I list in a quality of life statement?
- Would I include my family and loved ones? My business associates? What things would be important to them?
- If I were to write a personal creed or a focus statement, what would it say?

COURAGE — THE POWER OF ONE

Irène Laure was born in Marseilles, France.[3] The daughter of a businessman, Irène would steal her father's socks when she was a child to give to poor workers. She became a nurse and married Victor, who was a seaman and pupil of the French Communist leader Marcel Caching. In World War II, Irène was in the Resistance in Marseilles. After her son had been tortured by the Gestapo, her hatred reached a point at which she wanted every German to die and their country to be "wiped off the map of Europe."

At the end of the war, Irène was elected as a Member of Parliament and Secretary General of the Socialist Women of France. She later attended a conference in Switzerland that was aimed at restoring the unity of Europe. She was horrified to find Germans in attendance and at once packed her bag. Before she could leave, she was asked, "How do you hope to rebuild Europe without the Germans?"

Irène stayed for 3 nights of sleepless turmoil. Finally an internal voice told her to let go of her blinding hate. "I needed a miracle," she said. "I hardly believed in God, yet after days of agony, He performed that miracle. I apologized to the Germans, not for my resistance fight, but for having desired their total destruction."

Irène subsequently went to Germany and addressed 10 of the 11 German provincial parliaments. She spoke to hundreds of thousands in meetings and on the radio. Because of her, prominent Germans went to France and apologized on the radio and in the press to the French people for things that had happened during the war.

In the next years, several hundred leaders of the new Germany met with their French counterparts at Crux, Switzerland, and a tide of reconciliation was set in motion. The German Chancellor and the French Prime Minister said Irène Laure did more than any other individual to reconcile their countries after hundreds of years of enmity.

One Person Can Make a Difference

In the story of Irène Laure, we can find many attributes of authentic actions — acts of forgiveness, compassion, intuition, and courage — and the subsequent impact of these actions on the world. The point we stress is that first and foremost, Irène Laure changed the world by taking accountability for changing herself. Initially, when she stood in front of the provincial parliaments, her motivation appeared to be nothing more than achieving her own healing and commitment to service; she had no hidden agenda or motive to manipulate.

An adage of Mahatma Gandhi was "*Be* the change you wish to see in the world." By following this adage and courageously being the change we want in others, we make a decision to co-operate with the very source of creation. The universe welcomes and supports people who have the courage to lead — to grow where they are planted. By complaining or resisting or attaching blame, the life-force of being able to co-create a new outcome is blocked, and we remain entrenched in a self-made rut. By putting focus on ourselves instead of on "them," thus changing ourselves first, we will gain awareness that we can (and will) impact the lives of the people we lead.

Challenges to Being Courageous

Human nature likes to blame someone else. It was through conversations with Peter Block that we began to reflect on the notion that human nature appears to project onto others — particularly our leaders — the responsibility for achieving the qualities and expectations we are unwilling or unable to create for ourselves.

We abdicate personal accountability by blaming other people for things that we are not willing to change within ourselves. In the process, we renounce personal freedom. Impotence and helplessness emerge from blame as we continue, from a sense of entitlement and condemnation of other people, to forget that we are actually *co-creating* the very culture — whether it is in a relationship, an organization, a community — that we enjoy complaining about. And it seems we most enjoy blaming leadership.

Everyone is accountable, not just "management." Acknowledging that we have co-created the environment around us — and therefore we must be a part of the healing process — is the ultimate act of accountability. If we examine closely our expectations of leaders, and take accountability to initiate within ourselves what we expect from our leaders, we will transform our environment. In the process, we will find the freedom within that we have been seeking from our leaders. As Peter Block,[4] author, speaker, and consultant, so eloquently says, "The answer to how is yes."

A dichotomy appears to exist today. So many people want the world to "change" — they want more of something (e.g., love, money, etc.) or less of something (stress, conflict, etc.) so long as change is not required of them! Influential leaders of the future, regardless of position, will be people who have the courage to first transform themselves — by being dedicated to understanding "who they are" at a soul level and being willing to make changes, knowing that change must start within. As we have continually stressed in this book, to change the world, to change an organization, or to change a community or a relationship, start with yourself.

Authentic leadership, then, is letting go of the motive to "change" people, and replacing it with respecting, supporting, encouraging, and guiding people to be more of who they are. Only by traveling the path seeking authenticity will we be able to support their journey. We cannot give what we do not have!

Distrust is prevalent in the workplace. From research and observations of leadership across the country in a myriad of organizations during the past 5 years, we have found a prevailing distrust of leaders. This cynicism is emerging at all organizational levels of communities and governments.

Leadership development is at the end of the "flavor of the month" era, which has provided temporary, superficial leadership formulas. People yearn for leadership that eliminates gimmicks, rhetoric, and fads; leadership that is *real*. Based on our observations, this reaction to leadership is often justified, yet we also realize that seeing a lack of authenticity, a lack of leadership, or a lack of accountability in other people is always easier than seeing it in ourselves.

What Does Distrust of Leadership Really Mean?

Think about it. What are we saying about *ourselves* when we distrust our leaders? What are we saying about ourselves when we want our leaders to be more *real*? Do we trust *ourselves*? Are we waiting to have enough courage to become real for *ourselves*?

According to Peter Block, "There are inauthentic expectations. There is a distinction between what we are looking for in our leaders and an escape from our own freedom." This says that if we abdicate personal accountability by blaming other people for things we are unwilling to take personal responsibility for, in the process, we give up personal freedom. Complaining and an accompanying "entitlement" mindset becomes a reflection — or a statement — of our helplessness. Being focused on "those people" is a manifestation of a defensive stance concerning personal responsibility. The question, "How do we get *those people* to change?" or the statement, "*Those people* are doing such a lousy job of leadership" are distractions. They prevent us from choosing "who we want to become" and from exercising accountability for creating our own environment and lives.

Courage and Trust Are Powerful

Authentic leadership comes not from words. Authentic leadership comes from people *watching* you and *learning* from exemplary choices that you make. Trust, which is the foundation of leadership, is a result of first being trustworthy. Second, *self*-trust results from the courage — without blame — to take personal accountability for what is happening in your life. Nathaniel Hawthorne astutely wrote, "No person, for any considerable period, can wear one face to himself, and another to the multitudes, without finally getting bewildered as to which may be true."

The person we are will speak louder than any of our rhetoric.

INTEGRITY — THE POWER OF UNSHAKABLE CHARACTER

There is no real excellence in this world that can be separated from right living.
— David Starr Jordan

A troubled mother in India during the time Mahatma Gandhi was in office had a daughter who was addicted to sugar. One day she approached Gandhi, explaining the problem and asking if he would talk to the young girl. Gandhi replied, "Bring your daughter to me in 3 weeks' time and I will speak to her." After 3 weeks, the mother brought her daughter to Gandhi. He took the young girl aside and spoke to her about the harmful effects of eating sweets excessively and urged her to abandon her bad habit. The mother thanked Gandhi for this advice and then asked him, "But why didn't you speak to her 3 weeks ago?" Gandhi replied, "Because 3 weeks ago, I was still addicted to sweets."

As authentic leaders, we know we must do more than just "*point the way*" to other people — we must "*show the way*." The real power of leadership comes not from words, but from the integrity of our personal lives.

What Is Integrity?

Before continuing our discussion, consider these questions: What does it really mean to be a person who lives with integrity? What is the subsequent impact of integrity on a person and the people around them?

Integrity is from the word "integer," which means wholeness, integration, and completeness. This definition includes a sense of cohesion and congruence. Integrity is deeply personal and therefore deeply applicable to all areas of life. Integrity is the foundation of self-respect, which in turn is the bedrock of creating a respectful environment. Integrity leads to wholeness and integration and has a healing effect on the fragmented self that manifests itself by illnesses such as depression, anxiety, stress, and many other ailments that plague our modern-day world.

Integrity has three facets: self-honesty; honesty with other people; and accountability (the ability to be counted on). A commitment to having three-faceted authenticity — within oneself and with other people — is the beginning of strong *character*. A commitment to integrity allows us to have a "foundation" of authenticity, which is ownership of our own souls, making them unshakeable and not "for sale."

Having integrity affects our energy level, sense of aliveness and well-being, level of self-respect, and our health, while violating our integrity erodes our self-worth, life force, and connections. Taking a stand to have integrity will waken our energy no matter where we are. If we pay attention to maintaining integrity, we will see an immediate effect of integrity in our lives, relationships, and organizations.

Frustration, skepticism, fear, and suspicion are abundant in people, cultures, and relationships that lack integrity. Anyone who has been involved in situations in which people were dishonest, did not keep their word, or did not honor their promises has experienced first hand the effect of living without integrity. As an example, when a couple learned that their 14-year-old daughter had been stealing money from them, they were devastated to the point of utter despair. This sense of utter despair is what an integrity breach inflicts on a relationship and on the soul. It betrays the soul in the same way that stealing betrays our trust. In the case of this family, the betrayal of trust led to despair because it was so unexpected and out of the ordinary.

An Exercise in Integrity

The reverse is true when we have a *commitment* to being a person of integrity.

At this point, take a few minutes to participate in a short but potentially meaningful assignment. List the people that you can count on — without a shadow of doubt. When these people say they will do something, you *know* it will be done. Then reflect on the investment made by you and these people in the type of relationship that enables them to be on your list. When reflecting on these treasured connections, compare the effect of thinking about the impact these people have on your mind, body, and spirit with the effect of thinking about people that you *can't* count on. Notice the level of vitality and aliveness that results from even just *thinking* about the "connected" relationships. Earning the right to be on a person's integrity list is an extraordinary privilege. A relationship based on unequivocal integrity cannot be built overnight.

Next, if you want to take this assignment a step further, call the people on your list and tell them that they are on your list. Pay careful attention to the sense of aliveness that emerges during each conversation as you acknowledge their integrity and the meaning it has in your relationship.

To take this exercise a step farther, make a list of all the important people in your life. Then ask *them* to do this assignment. Ask yourself, honestly, "Will I be on their list?"

The Ripple Effect

Erosion of integrity in any area of life always has a ripple effect in every area of life. In the words of Mahatma Gandhi, "One cannot do right in one department of life whilst being occupied by doing wrong in any other department. Life is one indivisible whole." Dishonesty at work will affect our relationships at home, just as dishonesty in our personal lives will affect our contributions at work. A client once told us privately that he was having a supposedly "secret" affair with his secretary. At the same time, he had hired us to help his senior management group to become more accountable in their actions.

Taking a stand to have integrity in any area of life always has a positive effect on every other area of life. If you have ever had the opportunity (and privilege) to be in a room with recovering alcoholics, you have been a part of a culture of members committed to recovering their integrity.

By taking accountability to live honestly today, it is impossible *not* to have a desire to clean up the wreckage of the past. A commitment to integrity moves through the body, mind, and spirit, "flushing out" everything in its way. The same thing happens in organizations and in relationships. One person making a commitment to integrity impacts everyone around them. Integrity will *inspire* some people to move toward integrity — especially the people who are committed to living authentically. It will also cause non-authentic people to become resistant — particularly people who defend their right to live without integrity. The impact of taking a stand to have integrity cannot be denied. Ignoring the power of integrity is both naïve and unwise.

Integrity Is the Bedrock of Presence in Authentic Leadership

Bev Suek adamantly considers integrity to be essential for an authentic leadership presence. Relating her philosophy and approach to leadership, she says:

> From my work in organizations for many years, I have noticed that people will step over their line of integrity. Every time you "swallow" something that you don't believe in, you learn to swallow more. I have set my own line that I won't cross in terms of honesty and integrity, and I don't step over it. If it means I have to leave or do something different, then I leave and do something different. Nothing is more important to the foundation of my life than personal integrity. If you compromise your integrity, before you know it, you are learning to accept not having integrity. To me that has been one of the most important things in my career — being known as somebody who is honest and who keeps her word.

> Having worked for years in a political environment, I have been in numerous situations when people wanted me to do something that I didn't think was right... I have learned that there is a difference between people who feel that the end justifies the means and the people who believe that the means are just as important as the end. I happen to be one of those people.

... When I worked for Labour Canada, many people were counting the days until they retired. You know, they had 15 years and 73 days. Integrity wasn't important to them. They just did what they were told. They hated it, but they did it anyway. That's where it all started for me — when I made a decision that I couldn't lead my life that way. I had to do things that I believed in and in a way that I believed in. That's when I left government employment and started my own business. I wanted to do things in a way that I felt good about.

Integrity means having principles and doing what you say you're going to do. It's about being honest with yourself and others. It's about caring about things. It's not about doing things that you think are wrong. Even though lots of people seem to be able to do that, I think in the end we lose so much as a person that it's not worth it.

For Bev to sustain her integrity, energy, and self-respect, she once had to leave a place of employment. Yet, we have met people who have decided that to sustain their integrity, they had to *stay* in a job and change the environment through having the courage of their convictions. Each person must find their own way to live with integrity and to subsequently have authenticity.

Integrity Is Powerful

Remember: Integrity is not a demand for perfection or absolute clarity about issues. It is more about aiming for excellence than presenting an illusion of being flawless. Having integrity is having a commitment to invest deeply in the inquiry, to stay with the struggle, to continue to fight for what is right, and to *act* in accordance with the awareness that emerges. We have learned many things about integrity:

- It is better to under-promise and over-deliver than to over-promise and under-deliver.

- When taking a stand for integrity, the concern is not that it is *easy* or *hard*, but that it is *right*. The journey to unshakable character is choosing the *right* path over the *easy* path.

- Integrity results in self-respect. To build a respectful relationship, organization, community, or society, begin with *self*-respect that is a result of integrity.

- It is always easier to see a lack of integrity in someone else than to see it within ourselves. Rather than blaming others for a lack of integrity, use every experience of a breach of integrity by another as an inspiration for your recommitment to having personal integrity.

- A person is only as good as their word. After all, if a person cannot govern himself or herself, what else can they possibly govern?

Some Concluding Thoughts

In the movie *Gladiator*, Caesar explained to his general, Maximus, that Maximus would be the next leader of Rome. Maximus genuinely questioned this decision, asking Caesar why he was being chosen rather than Caesar's own son, Comitus. Caesar summed up the importance of integrity and delivered the message perfectly when he looked Maximus in the eyes and responded, "Comitus cannot rule. Comitus must not rule. For Comitus is not a moral man."

From the earliest days of the Rotarian organization, Rotarians promoted high ethical standards in their professional lives. One of the most widely printed and frequently quoted statements of business ethics is *The Four-Way Test,* created in 1932 by Rotarian Herbert J. Taylor when he took charge of a company facing bankruptcy. This 24-word test for employees became a business and professional guide for sales, production, advertising, and all relations with dealers and customers. The survival of the company was credited to this simple 24-word philosophy. Adopted by Rotary in 1943, *The Four-Way Test* has been translated into over a hundred languages, has been published thousands of times, and has stood the test of time as a valuable guide for making integrity-based decisions. *The Four-Way Test* asks four questions of the things thought, said, or done:

1. Is it the *truth?*
2. Is it *fair* to all concerned?
3. Will it build *goodwill* and *better relationships?*
4. Will it be *beneficial* to all concerned?

The Four-Way Test is a useful test of our commitment to integrity. Practice living the principles of integrity outlined in this section, weigh them carefully against the dictates of your conscience, and examine the results in your life.

SERVICE — THE POWER OF GIVING

It is one of the most beautiful compensations of this life — that no person can sincerely try to help another without helping themselves... Serve and thou shall be served.
— Ralph Waldo Emerson

The Mathare Valley is located on the edge of Nairobi, the capital city of Kenya. Amidst thousands of tin shacks, garbage is piled higher than a two-story house. There children, goats, and chickens congregate, eat, and play. In one of Africa's largest and poorest slums, for every 10,000 people, there is only one toilet, and the contents spill out into the paths between homes and into the small river where people bathe and wash their clothes.

An Unlikely Model of a Successful Organization

Underneath the apparent chaos, the Mathare Valley is a model of an organization in which the combined energy of 16,000 young people, mostly under age 18, has been harnessed to promote a youth culture that should be the envy of the world. Every Sunday afternoon, hundreds of children from the Mathare Valley descend on a football field at the SOS Children's Village in Nairobi that has been donated by the Federation International Football Association. Together with children who are cared for by the SOS Children's Villages, these children participate in football (soccer) leagues organized by the Mathare Youth Sports Association.

It All Started with Plastic Bags

The Association began in 1987, when Bob Munro, a Nairobi resident (and transplanted Canadian from St. Catharines, Ontario), watched children of Mathare playing football with a ball made of used plastic bags. Munro realized that sports, as a universal language, could be a way to empower the youth of the Mathare Valley. He took the idea a step farther by linking sports with service to the community. Together with Mathare residents, he started a small self-help project in which sports participation was linked to cleaning up the slum — and the Mathare Youth Sports Association (MYSA) was born.

In less than a decade, MYSA grew from one soccer team to more than 700 teams, giving 10,000 slum children an opportunity to play organized soccer. All Mathare United players complete at least 60 hours of community service each month, for which they are paid. Many of the players clean up the neighborhood as part of the MYSA Clean-Up Project. Some players go straight from practice to the Nairobi juvenile courts, where they help street children who have been arrested as vagrants. MYSA volunteers, working in conjunction with the Jamii Bora Trust, give these children food, help secure their release, and begin a process which often ends with the children being reunited with their families. Many team members are also trained HIV/AIDS counselors, spreading the prevention message in an area that is generally considered, due to poverty and ignorance, to be a high-risk area. MYSA now has over 200 youth leaders between the ages of 12 and 20 who have been trained in AIDS prevention and counseling.

It Grew from a Few People Convincing Other People to Give

Bob Munro, along with many associates, convinced other people that help was desperately needed in this community, and help has come their way in many forms. Soccer balls, clothing and shoes have been donated. Wheelbarrows, shovels, rakes, and a backhoe and garbage truck, a generous gift from the Norwegian Government, help remove garbage. Both small and substantial contributions are turning an entire community around.

Now MYSA Is Giving

In the Mathare Valley today, there is more self-esteem and more self-confidence, and even talk of Kenya's top soccer scorer who is a "graduate" of MYSA. According to Bob Munro, the Mathare Valley may not have changed much in appearance, despite the clean-up campaign, but the *people* have changed. The young people who run MYSA have an impressive amount of professionalism. There is no doubt that people at the top of the organization are having a major influence on the young people at the bottom. Children from the Mathare Valley begin life with the odds stacked against them. The road from slum boy to superstar is tough, to say the least. Yet, those who begin their sports careers with MYSA have shown that the combination of competition, discipline, community service, successful role models, and a desire to succeed, can produce the best in the business.

Commitment to a Cause Is a Powerful Force

The driving force behind all authentic actions is having a commitment to a cause beyond self-interest — having a dedication to serve other people. Great leaders throughout time have known this and lived by following the driving force of dedication to service. Dr. Martin Luther King, Jr. had a daily prayer that went, in essence, "Use me, God. Show me how to take who I am, who I want to be, what I can be, and what I can do, and use it for a purpose greater than myself."

Bob Munro's authentic leadership is fueled by a desire to serve and to make the world a better place. Authentic leadership compassionately inspires and guides other people to be the best they can possibly be. Our real legacy is the imprint we make on the lives of the people we impact.

Giving Is Required for Living

Service is at the core of authentic leadership. To live, we must give. Serving other people makes life worth living. Think about the Dead Sea. It has no outlet. It is stagnant and filled with salt. Yet, the Sea of Galilee is clear and clean and blue because the Jordan River disperses it to irrigate the desert.

Now think about your life and reflect on these questions: "What things make me the most proud?" "What accomplishments give me the most fulfillment or satisfaction?" Authentic leaders understand that at the end of our days, we can take no material things with us. The only things that we take are the things that we have given away. If we have helped other people, we take that with us. If we have given our time and money for the good of other people or for a worthy cause, we take that with us. If we have grown past self-centeredness, we take that with us. The things that inevitably give us satisfaction and inner peace are not what we have achieved or acquired for ourselves, but what we have done to make a difference for other people. This is what is really important in the long run.

When speaking about his father (the founder of Motorola), Bob Galvin describes his father's deep desire to be of service, a desire that inspires the actions of authentic leaders:[5]

> Dad once looked down an assembly line of women employees and thought, "These women are all like my mom — they have kids, homes to take care of, and people who need them." It motivated him to work hard to give women a better life because he saw his mother in all of them. That's how it all begins — with fundamental respect and a desire to serve.

John Charette, a career builder of communication bridges between jurisdictions and public service sectors, told us about having an early, deep-seeded passion and commitment for serving other people that was buried below a more obvious ambition:

> When I was in university, I was in a math/physics honors program. At that time, I was really determined to be a math professor. That was my goal in life. I was pretty good at math and did very well in my first year at university. I got something like 96% in math, so I guess that shows that I had the capacity to make that analysis or whatever.
>
> I got into the honors program, but found it wasn't quite what I thought it was going to be. It was a lot of work that centered around memorizing. I was dedicated to the

subject, but somehow it seemed to be *devoid of people* because it was all about ideas and things. I had never realized that. But, probably shortly after that, when thinking back about my school days, I realized that the thing that I enjoyed the most was *helping* other people to learn math. I had equated that with *learning* to be a mathematician, but what I loved most was helping people.

After a dismal third year in the honors program, I was led to work that was much more in line with my desire to serve…

The Concept of Leadership and Service

Servant-leadership is now in its fourth decade as a specific leadership and service concept. It is creating a quiet revolution in workplaces and communities around the world. This concept that first and foremost a leader is a *servant* derives from the experience of Robert Greenleaf, who spent a half-century working to shape large institutions. In the 1960s, his thinking was "crystallized" while reading *Journey to the East*, a novel by Hermann Hesse and an account of a mythical journey by a group of people on a spiritual quest.

The principal figure in the novel is Leo. Leo accompanies the party as the servant doing their menial chores, but he is also sustaining them with his spirit and his songs. Leo is a person of extraordinary authentic presence. All goes well until Leo disappears. Then the group falls into chaos and abandons their journey. They cannot continue without their servant Leo. The narrator in the novel is a member of the party. After years of wandering, he finds Leo and is taken into the Order that had sponsored the original journey. There he discovers that Leo, the person he had known as a servant, was in fact the Head of the Order, its guiding spirit and a great and noble leader.

Like all mythical stories, this novel is a tale of both a personal and a collective journey. Many interpretations are possible, but the tale demonstrates beautifully that authentic leadership is built on a core principle of service. Leo always was the leader, but he was a servant first. His commitment to service was the strength of his authentic presence and his impact on the group. The group bestowed the title of "leader" on Leo because of his impact on the group. Yet he was never there to "lead" — he was there to *serve*. This is who he was, deep down inside. And leadership emerged from this authentic internal place.[6]

Norm Augustine, an authentic leader dedicated to service above all, told us this:

> The quality of a leader that makes them genuine is self-lessness. I've known a lot of great leaders in my life and they not only suppress their self-interest for the good of the organization, their "self" doesn't even occur to them. They are people who are focused on the mission and not on themselves in any way. You're not much of a leader if people won't follow you. No one will follow someone they can't trust.
>
> A leader who suppresses self-interest has a strong interest in their people — they care about them — like in the military, the troops are fed before the officers. It's the little things that matter, but above all, it's about being genuine.
>
> In my experience, would-be-leaders, who always focus on their own successes, always, always fail. An inauthentic leader is constantly saying "How do I get ahead? How do I get what I want?" An authentic leader says, "How do I make sure we accomplish what we set out to accomplish? How can I help my people succeed?" It's a

certain irony that if you focus on personal success, you rarely achieve it. It's like the football player, the wide receiver who's running down the sidelines with 3 seconds left in the game, behind by 6 points. He's wide open with a forward pass coming toward him and he looks up in the stands to make sure everyone is watching and the ball hits him on the head. If you're too focused on being seen and getting credit for what you're doing, you usually make a mistake, you're distracted, and things don't work out.

I've been involved with many charitable organizations such as the American Red Cross and the Boy Scouts of America. Leadership there was quite different from when I was Chairman of Lockheed Martin Corporation. It's tougher to run a non-profit organization, because most of the people are volunteers and you don't get places by giving orders because everybody does what they do voluntarily. You don't have authoritarian lines of command. You have lines of willingness, and I think that is where leadership is more likely to be tested.

TRUST — THE POWER OF BELIEVING

The act of love is shown in no better way than through the act of trust.

—David Irvine

We will begin this section about trust with a story told by Doreen Finch:

When I was about 9 years old, my dad took me on a trip to visit his brothers and sisters in northern Alberta. I fell in love with the country and all my cousins who lived on the farm. Every summer, from then on, I insisted on spending the summer with Aunt Rose on the farm. Each July, as I packed my suitcase, my mother gave me a letter addressed to my aunt that essentially said, "Please don't let Doreen go to the barn or play with the horses or do anything dangerous." I dutifully took the note, put it in my suitcase, and dutifully gave it to Aunt Rose... on the last night of the summer before I returned home (which has always made Aunt Rose laugh).

During my visits to the farm, I developed a love of horses and riding. At the age of 10, I announced to Aunt Rose that I was going on a trip by horseback to see all my aunts and uncles who lived in the surrounding community. She looked at me with caution in her eyes because she knew that each of them lived 8 to 10 miles apart. She didn't say too much, so I reassured her that I would be okay.

I saddled up Queeny and put a roll on the back of the saddle with all my things in it. Each day, I would trek off on my horse feeling a sense of freedom and independence. On each trek I would arrive at the next farm. I was intrigued with my cousins and their lives. This was a very happy time for me.

My first stop took me to Uncle Alex's to spend a night or two. While doing chores with my cousins, we dreamed up skits to perform after supper. They still laugh at reunions and talk about the night I was all dressed up and danced with a broom.

When the time came for me to leave, everyone stood by, watchful and "guarded," while I saddled up Queeny and then rode off. Sometimes they would draw a map for me. They'd say, "Now when you get to this line, be sure to turn right, not left." The directions made the whole trip exciting. Having a map to follow made me feel like an adventurer.

My next destination was Uncle Lawrence's farm. Next was Aunt Alice's farm. Over 13 days, I visited 6 farms. They were all pretty concerned about a 10-year-old city kid getting on a horse and riding through country she'd never seen before, but never once did my aunts and uncles interfere. Never once did they say I couldn't go.

The last place was Grandma Carson's house. I loved Grandma Carson. She was from the Ozarks. She sat in a rocking chair on the porch and smoked a corncob pipe. I thought that was just the neatest thing in the world. My big ambition back then was to grow up and have a corn-cob pipe and sit on a porch just like Grandma Carson.

Queeny was a large pony with lots of spirit. Her gait was brisk, but her manners were good — until we were on the last leg of the trip and heading home. When Queeny knew we were homeward bound, I had to put my hands in the ring of the bit and hold her head right up against mine the whole way home. If I had ever given her a head, she would have gone into a full gallop. I would have been thrown off and left behind for sure.

When I arrived at Aunt Rose's farm from my journey around the country, I was so proud of my independence and grateful that I was trusted. I never found out, until years later, after I had grown up, that each time I left the yard of one of those aunts or uncles, a telephone call was made: "Doreen just left. She should be there in about 2 hours. Let me know when she gets there." Then, as I rode into each yard, before I got to the barn to unsaddle, a return telephone call was made to reassure the aunt who had made the call to say I was on my way. All along I thought I was on my own, but I know now that they were simply supervising from a distance, using a nice, healthy balance of support and trust.

This is a great example of letting people do what they can do on their own without interfering, but at the same time always being there as a backup. The whole experience gave me an enormous sense of accomplishment. I was a city kid who had never been on a horse. Taking this voyage on my own and having a message of encouragement and trust from the adults in my life made me feel like I was Gene Autry, Roy Rogers, and the Lone Ranger all wrapped up in one. I was the "King of the Road." The open air and freedom were life as it should be — exhilarating and a whole lot of fun.

Trust Encourages Self-Confidence

In Doreen's story, the experience of authenticity that trust encourages is abundantly seen. Yet, this story also eloquently describes the crucial value that an extended family has in providing leadership in a child's life. So often, grandparents, aunts, and uncles can provide this kind of trust more easily than a parent who has the everyday, ongoing responsibility of raising a child.

Lest we forget the credit due to Doreen's mother, she too exhibited courage and trust to support her young daughter by letting her find personal inspiration on a farm and letting her go to a place where Doreen loved to be. Her mother also nourished authenticity within her young daughter, even though she did not learn of Doreen's escapades on horseback until many years later.

Doreen gave some concluding thoughts about raising responsible young people with trust and confidence in our modern world:

> Children today are far too overprotected. We guard the many against the dangers of a few... The world is much better than the message we give to children today... It's too bad in this day and age that children are not encouraged to have a free spirit. They are so protected that when their parents get busy, they don't have time to teach their children how to deal with life's challenges. They don't have time to play with them or to bring them out of themselves.
>
> You can't help children find their spirit when they are in front of a television, being entertained, while their parents are busy doing what they have to do. Children need the support to learn to find their own adventures, for in adventures they will learn about who they are. The escapades I had on the farm could never have been found in front of a television. How will children today find their initiative?

At the age of 74, Doreen is speaking for the elders of our society, sages who have wisdom that can only be obtained from living and learning from experience. May Doreen's delightful story inspire you, not only to give the gift of trust to people you love and lead, but also to listen carefully to elders in our communities.

Authentic Leadership Encourages Trust

Authentic leadership is giving other people permission to have inner trust and be true to themselves. We are not leaders so that we can control or manipulate people. If we as leaders can create an environment where being true to self is consistent with being true to the workplace (or the place where they live), then we are doing the job of authentic leading. Perhaps the single most important thing we can offer to another human being is respect and recognition of the value of their uniqueness — not what they should be — but the worth of "who they are."

Consider how some people have expressed their views of trust in the work of leadership. First, Ian West:

> We don't "learn," we only "remember"… We are born with full knowledge. Our task is to "chip away" at our ignorance and forgetfulness. The "perfect being" is contained in a rock that is waiting for the ignorance to be chipped away to reveal "what God put inside."… When I work with people, I merely get a glimpse of the enormous, dormant potential there is inside everyone.
>
> This is where I make a distinction between religion and spirituality. Religion is a prescription given for an ailing soul. Spirituality is the spontaneous flow that prevents the ailment. The first is a response to sickness, while the second is an absence of illness.

Next is Eleanor Roosevelt, an authentic, transformational leader. She wrote:

> Every time you meet a situation, though you think at the time that [getting through] it is an impossibility and you go through the tortures of the damned, once you have met it and lived through it, you find that forever after you are freer than you were before.

Eleanor Roosevelt knew the power of trust from the depth of her own experience. You are freer because every time you meet a new situation and work through the journey, you come out of it as a person with more resources, more trust, and with a greater capacity to extend that trust to others.

Mike Crape describes trust in yet a different way:

> In building leadership, build the support you need by trusting others. When you trust and believe in people around you, you give them the power to make sure that you are staying true to yourself as well.

Trust Displaces Fear

In our experiences of working in communities and organizations across the continent and across cultures, we have seen how trust can displace the fears that separate people. Trust is the lubrication in relationships that makes questioning the motives of another person, looking for hidden meanings, or the need to have it in writing unnecessary. Because it is the foundation of all relationships, trust is the foundation of leadership. Relationships are more a function of trust than a result of technique.

When trust recedes, we are less open with one another and less interdependent, seeking outside help to assist us to interact, and look for protection from rules, policy manuals, and contracts. Erosion of trust and the subsequent growth of fear are the beginning of alienation, loneliness, and hostility — conditions that are becoming ever-prevalent in society. In a very real sense, our trust level is a thermometer of personal and relational health.

With trust, we function naturally and directly; we are able to become who and what we are meant to become; we let go and let other people in. Trust enriches life. We are more transparent, open, ready, and receptive. Trust frees creativity, allowing us to focus our energy on *building and discovering* rather than *protecting and guarding*. Trust releases tension, allowing the freedom to play, feel, enjoy, become angry, experience pain, and be who we are. Trust allows us to live spontaneously and unconstrained, which improves our energy, health, and overall well-being. Trust provides freedom.

As trust in oneself or in others diminishes, the void is filled with fear. Rather than directing energy to discovering and creating, the center of attention is on protecting and concentrating on how we *should* be rather than how we *are*. Fear that results from a lack of trust erodes our freedom by limiting our responses to life. Without trust, our energy flow becomes blocked. The result is tension, leading to one of three responses: withdrawal to safety; fighting back; or reverting to dependence on someone or something to intervene, such as a manager, rules, or an advocate (e.g., a union) for protection and direction. Each of these responses to a lack of trust blocks our potential and the expression of our own authentic self.

Authenticity and trust are inseparable. Trust provides an environment that fosters personal growth. To lead authentically and to be committed to creating environments where people can be at their best and where constraints and limitations are lifted, trust is essential.

Finding Clarity about Trust

We consider trust to have a number of characteristics. For us, the following brings clarity to an understanding of trust:

Confidence and trust are not the same. There is a difference between *confidence* and *trust.*[7] *Confidence* implies faith, perhaps because of some good reasons, definitive evidence, or from past experience. Confidence is more calculated and thought out. Confidence is based on expectations. For example, a leader might have *confidence* in a new leadership role if the leader already has similar leadership experience.

Trust is less strategic. Trust is more instinctive. Trust is similar to love because it can be freely given. The presence or absence of trust makes a powerful difference.

Consider a story about David's assistant, Laurie. Laurie received a request from her elderly parents to move with them to another province in Canada. At age 54, with her friends questioning her sanity, Laurie quit her job, moved two households to Vancouver Island, and opened up a business that was totally new to her. All the time, from somewhere deep within, she knew she would be okay because this is what she was "meant" to do. This is trust — the kind of quality that goes beyond mere confidence.

Later, when speaking about the move, Laurie said, "At this moment, my grandsons are here with me watching three deer munching moss on a rock cliff in front of my living room; a frantic rain is pounding against my windows while the fan-like leaves of my palm tree dance. I love my life more than I could ever have imagined... I know that I would never have been in this place, doing what I love doing and living where my heart is, without having a deep sense of trust."

Trust is a paradox. Trust presents a paradox in that it needs to be earned, but to be earned, trust must first be given. Trust, without some degree of confidence — or without having the facts on which to base it — is naiveté. This is the reason why trust is often given in small amounts over time. As we have success in trusting ourselves or other people, we become more willing to extend our trust. Yet, trust ultimately requires actions *despite* the risks. If we wait to have trust until there are no risks, then trust is not required. Trust is having the *courage* to step forward in the face of danger, knowing we can deal with the results.

Humans have a profound internal *knowing* that they can deal with life. Just as we are born "authentic," we are born to trust the process of life. Connecting to the trusting part of our nature is intricately connected to an authentic self and paramount in authentic leadership. To be trusted, we must first provide evidence that we are trustworthy with trustworthy behavior: honesty, sincerity, reliability, respect, transparency, congruence (where our words and actions match), dependability, and, of course, competence. Trustworthy behavior has trusting responses from others as an outcome.

Trust cannot be controlled, mandated, or legislated. Trust can only be invited by continuous and consistent trustworthy living. When stepping into a leadership role, do not expect trust from other people until it has been earned — through consistent, trustworthy behavior. When making "deposits in a trust account," remember to treat trust like a delicate flower. Years of making a "trustworthy investment" can be lost in a momentary, selfish act. For example, think of the trust built in a 40-year marriage. It can be broken in a single act of adultery. Trust has no shortcuts. Expecting trust to be gained by using shortcuts is naïve. Yet, trustworthiness, like authenticity, does not demand perfection. Trust is simply being perceived as a person worthy of earning trust — honest and willing to promptly admit when wrong or when making mistakes.

Trust begets trust; fear escalates fear. Trust is contagious. It inspires and develops trust in other people. Trust is self-fulfilling and makes the world a less dangerous place. Conversely, fear and distrust create more fear and distrust. This effect is obvious to people who spend time with animals, particularly horses. A rider who is fearful when getting on a horse will spark fear in the horse. The horse, then, reacts with fear, which in turn increases the rider's distrust for the horse — a self-fulfilling prophecy.

We know of a woman who worked in an organization where many of her colleagues had filed harassment charges against a certain manager. When asked if she was also being harassed (she was also a manager), she replied:

I have trust that that kind of thing just doesn't happen to me. People know I won't tolerate being treated like that. This is not a disrespectful environment for me. I give out trusting signals and I create my own environment.

She illustrates how the source of trust in a relationship is *self-trust*. People who are seeking authenticity are inspired by the courage of self-trust.

Trust is a choice, not a prerequisite. The first trust we experience is naïve and vital. It is the trust of infancy when babies reach outward into the world, knowing that the world will give them what they need. Somewhere between childhood and adulthood, the world does not "come through" for us, and the vital, innocent faith of a child is severed. From then on, we have a choice: to harden ourselves and withdraw from life's dangers, or find new resources that allow us to trust again with renewed strength and courage.

As adults, we *choose* to trust. Yet, after a betrayal, some people remain "non-trusting" for the remainder of their lives, hardening themselves with a protective shield of self-preservation, believing that the world is a non-trusting place, while never experiencing the growth that comes from real risk.

David's mother, Joyce, had this kind of self-trust. After witnessing years of abuse in her upbringing, Joyce experienced the pain of losing two husbands, one in World War II and a second from a brain aneurism after 35 years of marriage. In a conversation in her later years, Joyce spoke about how she learned to trust after such pain. "One thing's for sure — I'll not let anyone turn me into a non-trusting person. I trust people because I trust myself. And if I meet a person one day who is not worthy of that trust, then I'll trust myself to deal with it, no matter what it takes."

Joyce knew the depth of real and sustaining trust that comes from within, not from others. "Trust is a choice," she would say.

"And if you wait until it's safe to make that choice, you'll never trust, and you'll never see the fruits of the growth that trust brings." Shortly before her death Joyce spoke of the mystery before her. "I have no idea what I am walking into in my next experience, but I know that I will be okay. I trust." Within this deep knowing she had sustaining peace and left a most precious gift — the experience of her trusting spirit to walk into the mystery of life — and death — and to know of the power of this spirit.

Learning to trust other people begins with self-trust. As we work with organizations, communities, and families, people often tell us about problems of a lack of trust in their environments: tension, blame, stacks of policy and procedure manuals, defensiveness, hostility, cautiousness, and indirect communication. All of these are symptoms that indicate a lack of trust. Yet, when looking more deeply and really connecting with the people involved, we find excessive amounts of fear *inside* these people.

Instead of assuming that this finding was a result of the prevailing culture, we began with a belief that the lack of trust within the culture was the result of a lack of *self-trust*. Fearful people create a culture of mistrust, just as a culture of mistrust creates fearful people.

So we have returned to a primary premise of this book: To change a relationship — a work relationship, a marriage or lifelong partnership, or a relationship with a child — begin with yourself. By working on *yourself* and gaining self-trust, you will create a new environment. Trust is not a relationship problem as much as it is a problem that originates internally. Trust is an "inside job."

Some Final Thoughts

We believe that a universal life force — whether we are aware of it or not — is always working on our behalf, moving us toward growth, wholeness, and completeness. Just as a cut finger will heal without any act of will on our part, so too does the universe continually move us toward the growth and development of the soul — whether we are conscious of it or not. A key to authentic leadership, and a key to an authentic life, is realizing and understanding the power of this force.

Trust the process and trust the people you are leading. Authentic leadership is a shift from what *should* happen to what is *already trying* to happen. The place, whether it is a physical space or an internal place, is an environment in which the soul can grow and flourish. We can find this space by letting go of things that we think *ought to be* happening. In so doing, we will discover expanded attentiveness to the things that are already trying to happen spontaneously. This space supports the growth of our own souls because it is a trusting environment. This space is also essential to inspire and support growth in other people. For us, this is true in retreats we facilitate, organizations we have run and consulted with, and in our families.

HUMILITY — THE POWER OF AN HONEST IDENTITY

You can accomplish anything in life, provided that
you do not mind who gets the credit.
—Harry S. Truman

Jim Collins has rigorously studied great companies.[8] He carefully researched the type of leadership that was required to take a company from "good" to "great." He had meticulous criteria for greatness, which had to be sustained over a 15-year period. After 5 years of painstaking analysis, the histories of 28 companies were thoroughly examined. After sifting through mountains of data and thousands of pages of interviews, Collins and his research team discovered the key determinants of greatness — why some companies make the leap and others do not. In all of the "great" companies, *humility* was a vital leadership quality. *Humility* in leaders is manifesting a compelling *modesty* — a desire to *not* talk about themselves, to *not* draw attention to themselves, and an accompanying compelling desire to give other people the credit for accomplishments.

What Is Humility in a Leader?

Humility in a leader can be described by words such as *quiet, humble, modest, reserved, shy, gracious, mild-mannered, self-effacing, understated, and "did not believe his own clippings"* — adjectives also used to describe "great" leaders.

Consider Collins' story of board member Jim Hlavacek describing Ken Iverson who oversaw the transformation of a company from near bankruptcy to being one of the most successful steel companies in the world:

> Ken is a very modest and humble man. I've never known a person as successful in doing what he's doing who is as modest. And I work for a lot of CEOs of large companies. That's true in his private life as well. It's the simplicity of him. I mean little things. He always gets his dogs at the local pound. He has a simple house that he's lived in for ages. He only has a carport and he complained to me one day about how he used his credit card to scrape the frost off his windows and he broke the credit card. "You know," I said, "there's a solution for it; enclose your carport." And he said, "Ah, heck, it isn't that big of a deal." He's that humble and simple.

None of the great leaders identified in Collins' research ever aspired to be larger-than-life heroes. Great leaders do not want to be put on a pedestal or become an unreachable icon. They are seemingly ordinary people who are quietly producing extraordinary results, with a ferocious resolve to do what needs to be done to make their organization great.

This description of modesty was completely in line with every person we interviewed for this book. From all the leaders we interviewed, their first response was, "Why would you pick *me* for an interview about authentic leadership? I don't see myself as any kind of an authentic leader." It was evident they had no aspirations to be heroes. They were simply doing what they loved to do, bringing that spirit forward in a spirit of generosity and service. The compelling quality of modesty appears to be a determinant for why people were drawn to these leaders.

Humility Is Powerful

Being around people with humility, who have a degree of inner confidence that makes dependence on arrogance for security unnecessary, is compelling and powerful. It is invigorating to be with a person who does not attach their well-being to knowing, but rather is open to learning. Humility is a true evaluation of conditions "as they are," a willingness to face the facts, seek the truth about themselves and their environment, and honestly seek an accurate perception of current reality. Humility leads to self-searching and is a means for bringing new vision and actions to the darker side of human nature. Humility is anything but weakness.

Authentic leaders see themselves as facilitators of people's full potential. They know their ability as a leader does not diminish when other people "shine" because they are aware of the true source of their ability. Authentic leaders are not afraid of another person's competency. Instead, they honor other people.

Humility Earns Respect

Bev Suek expressed the importance of earning respect through humility:

> To lead, you have to recognize that humility is an impor-
> tant part of what you do. You are not as smart as you
> sometimes think you are. A CEO or a person who is sur-
> rounded by CEOs will have a really hard time not get-
> ting caught up in thinking that they are the most
> important person in the whole world. I really have to
> keep reminding myself that everybody has something to
> contribute. It's not just me…
>
> I started an organization years ago called Kali Shiva. Our
> son died of AIDS. He inspired us to eventually start an
> organization to help others who had AIDS. As an orga-
> nization, we set up teams of volunteers to work with
> AIDS patients who wanted to stay at home as long as
> they could or wanted to die at home. June Menzies was
> one of our volunteers. June used to head up the
> Economic Council of Canada. I was always in awe of her.
> And now here she was, joining Kali Shiva as a volunteer.
> June's job was to pick up patients' laundry, wash it, and
> take it back to them. Everybody at Kali Shiva thought
> that June was the "laundry lady." She never corrected
> them. June never said, "Really, I used to be head of the
> Economic Council of Canada."

Bev continued:

> I've always aspired to be a "laundry lady." To me, that
> kind of humility is something leaders ought to strive for.
> They don't need recognition or acclamation from others
> because it's internal. It's part of who they are. They

already feel good about themselves. That's always been my inspiration — to be the laundry lady and not have to tell people that I'm wonderful and great and important.

Another interview was also a good example of humility in action. When we asked Ray Taillefer how he accounted for his successes, he was quick to attribute his accomplishments to other people:

First, I give credit to the love from my mother and father who had little materially, but the patience of my father and the generosity of my mother encouraged me. Next, my wife gives me confidence, support, and unending love in pursuit of what I think is right. She has a capacity to keep me grounded... I also give credit to the amazing people who surround me today, in both my business and my personal life. The foundation of my life is my faith, and the faith that others have in me and I in them. God is always with me...

It's important to never take yourself so seriously that you forget your roots and forget about humility. Leadership is putting ego and power aside and respecting people and being willing to hear about things you don't want to hear about. Oftentimes, that's one of the most important things you need to do as a leader.

Humility Is an Openness to Learn

Authenticity is being "teachable" and taking risks to be open to learning. Not only is humility a virtue of authentic leadership, it is also described by many people as being a *spiritual* virtue. Humility is a product of your identity — being free from self and being willing to strive for purposes that are beyond self-interest and self-will.

Some people may view humility as a weakness, for they do not see the enormous courage and strength below the surface of a modest, self-confident individual with a firm persuasion. Anything but weak, humility is a "quiet place" where you can keep enough perspective and enough balance to take the next right action that will be aligned with what matters.

The attainment of greater humility is the foundation of authentic leadership, of influencing others with presence over position. But humility is not just a virtue of authentic leadership. Many would describe humility as a spiritual virtue.

Ben Wong and Jock McKeen gave us another consideration of humility:

> One of the difficulties we have found is that it's appealing to people to think they can achieve some awareness of their authentic self. The danger is in making an authentic self a role of its own. We ourselves are afraid of getting caught up in the role of an authentic being, so we want to make sure we don't make that our goal.
>
> We first ran into this in the 1960s during the hippie revolution. Hippies were in search of their authentic selves. We actually had a great belief in their goals. At one time, I was even described as being a "hippie shrink." But the hippies made a rule that in order to *be* authentic, you had to be in old blue jeans and an outdoor lumberman's shirt. Those were the only authentic beings.

Jock McKeen added, "It was a simulation of authenticity and became a bit of snobbery — 'I'm more authentic than you are.'"

Some Final Thoughts

In some ways, our approach to leadership can be accurately measured by our degree of adherence to the standard of humility. Humility is one of the touchstones for the growth and development of the soul and the people we serve. Humility is the very essence of right *being* and right *doing*.

COMPASSION — THE POWER OF LOVE

Good leadership is largely a matter of love. Or if you're uncomfortable with that word, call it caring, because leadership involves caring for people, not manipulating them.
—James A. Autry

No matter how much wealth we accumulate, possessions we have, titles or academic degrees behind our name, or positional power held in a community or organization, one question puts everyone on even ground. This question strips away all the trappings and innumerable ways we use to define ourselves in this world. This one question — with three words — cuts to the core of being human: *Are you loved?*

Authentic Leadership Is from the Heart

The essence of authentic leadership, of having impact from the strength of our presence, is reaching people at their "heart" level, being compassionate. Having compassion is another vital quality of authentic actions.

Compassion means to "feel with," to open yourself to the vastness of the human experience so you can tune in to the inner life of those you serve. When we lead solely with tools and techniques it is easy to forget that we are dealing with people who have needs, feelings, and concerns. People are not objects that participate in some well-conceived design. Authentic leadership is about *people*, and what we bring to this work of leadership when we are committed to make a lasting difference is a willingness and ability to connect with people so our conversations are meaningful and truthful. Think about this question: Whose needs are being met when we align systems, redesign work, and reorganize a culture? Whenever a sense of someone *doing* something to *someone* exists, a "red flag" should go up. Unless we have deep respect, compassion, and willingness to engage in learning together, how collaborative can a process be? Let's face it, when asked about our work as consultants and leaders, it is much easier to talk about the latest strategic planning session or most recent project management process than to describe a meaningful conversation.

Compassion in the Workplace

Consider some examples of compassion in the workplace. The first example comes from a conversation with Ray Taillefer who spoke to us about compassion and love when describing succession in his family business:

> If you really believe in succession, you'll understand that it's a "love story." I describe it as a love story because in order to succeed at succession, you have to be in love with the greater good of your family, your business, and of what you are all working toward... It's this love that gives me the strength, every day, to step back, keep my ego out of the business, and make "room" for my sons and employees... But if you miss it and forget why you're doing it, you'll never carry out succession. That's what I've learned. It's like you'd better say your prayers every night to have the strength to do it...

Next is the example of Jim DeMesa who spoke frankly about the importance of compassion in his practice, first as a physician and then as a CEO:

> When I was first practicing as a young physician, just out of residency, I seemed to somehow know instinctively when I saw patients who were really sick or who seemed concerned or worried or who had health conditions that concerned me. I would take a little time to put the charts aside and just sit with them. I'd often call them the next day and ask, "Hey, how're you doing? Are you feeling any better? Are you having any reactions to the medications?"
>
> The response I got both directly and indirectly from them was unbelievable. They would refer people to me and when I'd meet these new patients, they'd say, "Yeah, I heard that you care so much about your patients that you call people at home and ask them how they're doing after you've treated them." And I'd say, "Well, it's just part of the treatment."
>
> It was all about relationship building. People responded dramatically and my practice got very successful because of that. I don't think I was giving any better medical care than any of my colleagues. I was just doing what came naturally to me. Being with people in this way is my barometer for knowing when I'm on track as a leader. I'm connected to people and people feel they're connected to me. Now as a CEO, I've asked my director of HR, in preparation for this interview, to give me some specific perspective about my leadership. It is part of our culture here to give each other feedback regularly. She responded by saying, "People feel that they can come

and ask you anything and challenge you with anything. It's not taboo at all. In fact, it's quite comfortable."

I think that when people can connect, progress is made. If they can't connect with me, they couldn't ask me questions like, "Why are we doing this?" They couldn't say, "I don't agree with this." They would keep that inside. I think that's counterproductive and can eventually destroy an organization.

Now, reflect on compassion in your life and work. How much room do you make to open your heart, reflect deeply on what matters, and really care about what is going on in your environment — beyond completing to-do lists and meeting agendas?

Compassion Is Not Always Being Efficient

Compassion allows us to have a sense of *grace*, to live our lives more fully and to give ourselves time, for a child, a loved one, an employee — or to work in your garden or watch a sunset. Compassion is a way of "being" in the world. It lights the fire of connection — connection to loved ones, to the community, to a purpose beyond ourselves, and to the hidden self that we rarely bring to an environment that is driven by efficiency and ambition.

Have you ever tried to be "efficient" with a loved one, an employee, or a customer when they simply needed a small amount of our attention? As we connect more fully in life, we become more attuned to people we care about. Compassion allows a renewed understanding of our environment, and the beauty and depth of each human being that may be missed in our busyness.

Compassion Is Being Respectful

Chuck Williams shares his deep respect, once again, for the leadership qualities of Bill Hewlett and other members of senior management at HP. He offers a story that illustrates how compassion can also be expressed as simple respect for another person and a commitment to the development of their spirit:

> I left HP in the late 1970s to pursue other avenues. Some people viewed this type of move quite negatively. One simply did not leave "the tent." Consequently, when I resigned, I did not hear from some people with whom I had worked closely over the years.
>
> But I did hear from many others, including senior management. Bill Doolittle, then Senior Vice President of International Operations, flew to Toronto to have dinner with me and tell me I would be welcome to return. Bob Boniface, then Executive Vice President of Marketing, wrote to thank me for my contributions to HP and to wish me well. Bill Hewlett wrote to congratulate me on the progress we had made at HP Canada, finishing by saying, "I'm sorry you are leaving, but I completely understand your desire to spread your own wings."
>
> To me, these people embody the very essence of leadership.

A Concluding Question

Have you noticed that all of the characteristics of authentic action are interdependent? None of them can be expressed or developed in isolation from the rest. Compassion, to take root, must be grounded in strength of courage, clarity, and integrity and anchored in a firm resolve to remain true to clear and abiding principles.

VULNERABILITY — THE POWER OF BEING HUMAN

In the right place, at the right time, in the right way, your greatest strength as a leader is your vulnerability.
—David Irvine

The image of leadership today is no longer an outdated version of someone on a horse "leading the charge," but rather something much more recognizable and something much more challenging. The image of great leadership today is of a person who has a capacity to create engaging, life-changing, and meaningful *conversations*. To assess your current capacity as a leader, look carefully at the quality of your conversations.

Reflect on these questions in relationship to your leadership and the people you currently serve and want to impact:

- Do we talk to each other about important matters?
- Do I spend time talking "to" people or do I connect "with" people?
- Do my current conversations inspire, uplift, and engage me? Or do they deplete me?
- What is the level of honesty and openness in my current conversations?
- How well do I clarify my expectations and agreements with other people?
- Am I able to inspire and lead others toward a shared vision?

Qualities of Authentic Conversation

Authentic conversation is based on two qualities:

- Have compassion. Treat people as real persons, not just as a means to an end or an asset to accomplish an objective.

- Be vulnerable. Vulnerability is a capacity to be more fully human. Real conversation requires a significant degree of vulnerability.

For years, the belief about leadership included possessing a type of "armor" or a pretense of "knowing," and the subsequent expectation of leaders to present their best side. But we are learning that leading with sustained impact requires more than a "best side." Authentic leadership requires listening emphatically and observing the process, and knowing ourselves enough to be aware when our own need for acceptance and approval gets in the way. Meaningful conversation requires understanding ourselves and our environment. To know ourselves, we must step away from the identities that we so tirelessly create and embrace the unfamiliar.

Connecting Requires Vulnerability

Connecting with other people at the "soul" level requires having a level of vulnerability in which we are appropriately open about our uncertainties, mistakes, and the normal ebb and flow of life. Authentic people are compelled to be vulnerable because vulnerability is real. Owning up to one's weaknesses and showing humanness in a leadership role is persuasive. Vulnerability made Winston Churchill endearing: "The key to life is to go from one failure to the next without a loss of enthusiasm." Empowering people to own up to their weaknesses is very powerful.

Vulnerability Is Powerful

What if we always present ourselves in the best possible light? It would be like watching a movie that has no conflict or tragedy — a dull and disengaging experience. Think about it. If everyone presented themselves as "having it all together," who could we believe? People are drawn to a more realistic picture of life experiences. To connect more fully with other people, the characteristic of vulnerability — which is part of a whole self — is important. Authentic leaders are appreciative of vulnerability and humanness and value it.

Judy Walton spoke frankly about vulnerability in leadership. Her story is powerful:

> Most of the "aha moments" I have had in my life, that have important application to my work organizations, have been the gifts of having perspectives that usually require some kind of personal challenge or problem. One such challenge was being with my husband while he was dying. He was very ill for a period of 2 to 3 years and ultimately died… The gift in that kind of an experience is that you get reminded on a real-time basis of what's important in life. It makes you able to distinguish some of the things that can take on too much magnitude in organizations at times. I'm not grateful for the experience, but I'm grateful for the lessons that this experience provided. I'm also grateful for what I learned from him as he went through that experience.

> What I learned from it, among other things, was that dying was a great reminder of the vulnerability that we all have. And it was a great reminder about compassion.

> Death magnifies awareness. It really does. One of the things that I try to remind myself is not to forget this lesson. Sometimes as grief fades, the lesson fades… To keep

> the lesson alive, I try to recall some of the clarity I had
> then and what was happening and how it's valuable and
> keep the good parts with me...

Personal insight and understanding do not come easily. Finding them requires deep reflection. In addition to personal reflections, engage in conversations with friends, mentors, and confidants who will hold up a mirror and provide honest feedback. Creating an environment for good conversations that generate insight and understanding is a lifelong journey.

Vulnerability Is Being Courageous

Consider the comments of Patty Woods. Her thoughts are about the importance of vulnerability and expressing it by having the courage to be "who one is":

> I made a choice a while back that I was going to be who
> I was. If that meant I told people how much I cared
> about them, if I hugged people, if I signed "love" on a
> card, if I gave little thank you gifts, or if I was overt
> about inner personal conflict, then that was going to be
> the way I wanted to be as a manager.
>
> I think I was always worried that I would be "found out"
> as being quite an emotional person, but that is my style
> as a manager and that is okay.

Vulnerability Is Expressed in Many Ways

Vulnerability, like all other qualities of authenticity, can be expressed in a variety of ways. Jim DeMesa discussed vulnerability from a perspective of having a commitment in the workplace to foster a culture of open communication and connection:

A big part of relationships is communication. So one of the things that I think about is, "If I were being led, how would I want to be led?" I'd want open dialogue. So I kind of force that in a variety of ways. I force it from the perspective of creating a culture of communication and a trusting environment. I schedule time every single month to have an all-company meeting. It can last for an hour and a half, or it can last 4 hours.

People sometimes say, "I don't have time for this." I respond by saying, "There's no time to not do this." I also set up all kinds of scheduled meetings where it's a little more personal — smaller groups, at random, with people throughout the company. They volunteer for these meetings so we'll talk a little more intimately, from a professional standpoint and to a certain degree a personal standpoint. We talk about things like, "What's exciting right now, what's challenging, and what's frustrating? How can we improve these things?"

In these connections, the more open I am with them, the more these people will be open with me. It's leadership by example...

Vulnerability in Authentic Leadership

Vulnerability is a quality that sets authentic leaders apart. Vulnerability is a capacity to lead communication and foster connections by being open and honest. We will end this section by listing some keys to vulnerability and its importance in authentic leadership:

- Vulnerability is a path to intimacy, but it is also a path to creating a culture of trust, which is the foundation of sustained productivity.

- A capacity to be vulnerable and transparent comes from having deeper inner qualities — confidence, self-awareness, and humility.

- Vulnerability at any given time depends on several variables: confidence level, degree of inner peace, and trust in the people in our environment. Being vulnerable is easier during periods of being less "needy." Insecurity tends to cause us to "play it safer" or "do it the way everyone else does it."

- People want to know the truth. They may not always be comfortable with the truth, but it is human to want to learn. No one wants to learn things that are distorted or untrue.

In conclusion, we have two cautionary suggestions about vulnerability:

First, vulnerability cannot be controlled, legislated, or mandated. Vulnerability can only be *invited*. This is not a "technique" for getting people to open up. It is a process that emerges authentically from within, which allows us to engage in meaningful dialogue. Vulnerability is not to be expected from others. It is something to be *lived*.

Second, before being vulnerable, carefully examine your motives. If the intent is to serve and to build a relationship and foster an open, trusting culture, being vulnerable cannot be too far wrong. The danger is in turning vulnerability into another leadership technique.

Think About This

Oscar Wilde once said, "Once you can fake sincerity, the rest is easy." Faked sincerity may last for a while, but shallow veneers soon wear thin.

ENDNOTES

1. *The Box*. Adapted from Therma Collective of Nepal. Available at: http://www.iloveulove.com/spirituality/follow-heart.htm.

2. Allan Savory. 1999. Adapted from *Holistic Management*, pp. 69–85. Washington, DC: Island Press.

3. Initiatives of Change, adapted from a website that has stories about people around the globe who are changing the world by *being* the change they wish to see in the world. Available at: www.iofc.org.

4. We are indebted to Peter Block, author of *The Answer to How Is Yes: Acting on What Matters* (2002, San Francisco: Berrett-Koehler); *Stewardship: Choosing Service Over Self-Interest* (1996, San Francisco: Berrett-Koehler); and *Freedom and Accountability at Work: Applying Philosophic Insight to the Real World* (co-author, Peter Koestenbaum) (2001, San Francisco: Pfeiffer), for his wisdom, perspective, and generosity in developing our thinking about authentic leadership. We highly recommend any of Peter's superbly written books. Any leader who is committed to authenticity and accountability in leadership is well advised to have these books on the top shelf of a library for employees to borrow.

5. Gay Hendricks and Kate Ludeman. 1996. *The Corporate Mystic: A Guidebook for Visionaries with Their Feet on the Ground*, p. xix. New York: Bantam Books.

6. Larry Spears and Michele Lawrence, Eds. 2002. *Focus on Leadership: Servant-Leadership for the 21st Century*. New York: Wiley & Sons. This book contains essays on servant-leadership by prominent people in the leadership development field, including Warren Bennis, Stephen Covey,

Margaret Wheatley, and John Bogle, and provides a more in-depth understanding of servant leadership.

7. Jack R. Gibb. 1978. Adapted from *Trust: A New View of Personal and Organizational Development.* Los Angeles: Guild of Tutors Press. Jack Gibb has had an enormous impact on our thinking about trust.

8. Jim Collins. 2001. *Good to Great: Why Some Companies Make the Leap... and Others Don't.* New York: HarperBusiness.

CHAPTER 5

Strategies For
Strengthening Your
Authentic Presence —
Making Authenticity
Real

Sow a thought and you reap an act;
Sow an act and you reap a habit;
Sow a habit and you reap a character;
Sow a character and you reap a destiny.

—Makepeace Thackeray

Authentic leadership begins by recognizing and understanding "what's going on inside you." *Being* authentic in leadership *invites* authenticity. If the real impact on other people is not from our position, but from our presence, then how is stronger authentic *presence* developed?

We began to wrestle with this question many years ago. Time and experience have provided us with some clarity.

173

This chapter will describe some practical strategies for *getting on* a path of authenticity and then *staying on* it, thus amplifying your personal impact on other people by having a stronger presence.

Before reading our list of strategies, consider Jerry Weinberg's comments about developing presence. He says:

> I don't think a person can develop the power of their presence by *trying* to develop it. Giving someone advice about developing authenticity is like giving advice about how to find a spouse. Rather than trying to find a spouse, "just try to be the person that the person you want to be with wants to be with too."

> The kind of person I want to be with has similar values and acts on them and lives by them, instead of just talking about them. If a person tries to live by their values, they become the kind of person who has the same values as the people who are naturally drawn to them...

> You don't become an artist by putting on a beret and sitting in a café just because artists do that. There's a lot more to it. You have to work on yourself, on the art of *being* yourself, and when you do that, other people — at least the people you want to be around — will find it compelling.

> Other people might be repelled, but that's good, because you don't want to be around them anyway. A good part about being a leader is not wasting time on people you don't want to lead and on people who don't want to be led in the direction you want to go in. You can stop dragging people around and start facilitating common values in action.

This is what I have come to in the later part of my life. I'm getting better at being me. When I do this, some people might *see* me as a leader, and take a lead from me, but I don't set out to *be* a leader. I just set out to be better at being myself.

GUIDELINES FOR AUTHENTICITY

As described by Jerry, we would not want anyone to *try* to be authentic, but we will describe a few guideposts that hopefully will help you keep your intention of having a stronger authentic presence at the forefront. When reading the list, remember that all of us are unique and that our needs will change over time. Some people might be at a stage when authenticity means being *more* vulnerable, receptive, and connected, but *less* independent. For others, authenticity may mean being *more* independent and autonomous. Some people need structure and action, while others need to get away from planning to make room for reflection and stillness, simply for *being*. Each of us has a personal approach to the important matters of life.

When considering new methods, respect your existing methods. Remember: Respect yourself. Do not be compelled to apply all of the strategies, especially not all at once. Consider our list to be a smorgasbord of ideas. You might even want to write a personal list. For now, take methods from our list that are a fit and leave the rest. Yet, keep an open mind. Some of the methods you left off today might have more relevance at a later date.

Also, we suggest that you take time to transform the suggested strategies into *habits*. From within the seeds of habit character is harvested. Everyone has habits. The important questions are, "What are yours?" and "Where are they taking you?" From experience, we know that the guidelines outlined in this chapter can be life-changing when taken to the level of daily actions.

Now we will move on to discussing some practical strategies for embarking on a path of authenticity and achieving a strong presence, and then staying on it, to amplify our personal impact on other people.

STEP OUT OF THE FRAY

To be authentic, leadership requires action *and* reflection. We must alternate between contribution and examination, something described by Walt Whitman as being "both in and out of the game."[1] For example, a great athlete such as Wayne Gretzky attained greatness in hockey in part from an ability to play hard, while simultaneously keeping his mind on the entire game situation, as if he were sitting in the stands. This is a capacity that is much easier described than done.

Consider how easy it is to be swept away by events in our environment rather than maintaining perspective. Anyone who has learned a new skill — from golfing to public speaking — recognizes that engaging in a new activity makes observing quite difficult. Anyone who is developing or improving a skill understands the importance of first stepping *into the action* and then stepping *back from the action* to observe, reflect, and learn.

How can we step away from the fray to gain perspective on the events that continue to surround us and seem to sweep us away? Answering this question is a significant theme in all the remaining strategies for strengthening presence.

SET ASIDE DAILY QUIET TIME

The velocity of human experience has become so accelerated that our capacity to sustain contemplation is being eroded. Reconnecting with our authentic selves begins with recognizing times when our constructed selves and our authentic selves are incongruent. It is within the quiet moments that we may first begin to feel the discomfort of misalignment.

Authenticity — from which presence emerges — requires that we slow down and make room to contemplate, reflect, and have ongoing self-examination. An authentic presence cannot take root in the depleted soil of frantic busyness. Making daily quiet time a habit is the beginning of the practice of "going within." Staying busy is a protective mechanism to avoid the discomfort of facing ourselves. At first, quiet time may be uncomfortable, but stay with it. Seeking the truth about oneself requires listening to the promptings of the heart. Sifting through layers of illusion, blame, victimhood, fear, and manipulation necessitates making room for stillness — on a consistent basis.

By daily making time available for solitude, silence, and attending to the voice within, we begin to walk an authentic journey. On a regular basis, begin some form of spiritual practice — meditation, prayer, or simply taking time to relax.

To *impart* our full authentic presence and the gifts that emerge from that presence, we must step *apart* from the world to discover who we are. Find a practice that is a fit, become a student of that practice, and stick to it.

FIND A PERSONAL SANCTUARY OR CREATE ONE

Listening to a deeper voice from within requires having a place where the deeper voice can be heard. Many voices have access to us today: advertising, the media, customers, solicitors, clients, bosses, well-meaning friends, extended family members, children, and community members, to name just a few. When living amidst the many voices that demand attention, our voice is easily lost. A place must be reserved — a sanctuary — where technology can be turned off and we can be alone to hear ourselves think. A sanctuary is a place for retreat from the world's demands, where solace and serenity can be found and the whisper of our own voice can be heard.

A sanctuary is formally defined as a sacred place; the holiest part of a temple; the part of the chancel containing the altar; an area where wild birds and animals are protected; and a refuge. In practice, sanctuaries are very personal. A sanctuary is a haven, a place to step away from demands of the world, a designated place to contemplate, relax, and "just let it be."

Claiming a sanctuary is part of human nature. Wanting to regularly retreat is innate and necessary. It is vital to give ourselves permission to seek sanctuary and trust our instincts to create and use a place of solace. We find untapped resources by consciously developing our external and internal sanctuaries.

Create a personal sanctuary for quiet time. For some people a sanctuary is a religious place, a formal institution. For others, a sanctuary is a kitchen table or a jogging trail or a special bench where they sit by a quiet river or underneath beautiful trees. When traveling, we can find peace in the sanctuaries of airport chapels. Every major airport has one. Airport chapels are rarely used, but they are wonderful, peaceful places in the demanding, stressful world of travel.

Most hospitals have chapels and sanctuaries. In cities across the world, churches, synagogues, and mosques open their doors at noontime. Some business executives eat their lunch and then sit quietly in a church for the remainder of lunchtime. They are drawn to churches, not necessarily for religious reasons, but because churches provide a place for stepping back from the noise of the world where they can "go within."

TAKE TIME TO RETREAT

We know a CEO who participates yearly in a silent retreat in a monastery near his community. From Friday afternoon until Sunday afternoon, he sits in a community of people who maintain silence for 48 hours. Another man joins the First Nations elders in his community yearly for a sweat and 4-day fast. We regularly attend courses that are away from the routines of life as a way to reconnect with the deeper parts of ourselves.

Make a habit, in whatever way that connects you with your soul, to regularly and consistently "step out of the fray" and engage in important questions to gain perspective, insight, fellowship, and deepened competence in your practice of authentic living.

PAY ATTENTION

Part of the process of slowing down and making room for reflection is to apprentice ourselves to the art of *paying attention* — internally and externally. Everyone experiences times that are hectic and demanding and cause us to overly focus on reacting to external stimuli. Too often, quality is squeezed out of life. We contribute to the lives of other people, but are losing contact in our own lives. Sometimes we are so busy putting out fires in our environment that we do not make time to rekindle the fires of our inner lives. One day, looking inside, we notice our own fire is out.

What happened? Needing to react to society's demands, we have neglected to respond to desires of the soul. Life has become too much like being on a boat in which all the oarsmen are pulling in different directions. Learning to connect with and listen to our inner voice, and then following the promptings that emerge, develops the fine-tuned instrument we need to reach, inspire, support, and guide people we serve in our work of leading.

MONITOR PERSONAL ENERGY

Monitoring our energy levels in response to our environment develops the skill of paying attention. Pay attention to the energy levels that result from our responses to music, television programs, the office building where we work, people we spend time with, food we eat, the photographs and images in our homes, our neighborhoods, our back yards, and the vehicles we drive. Notice how some environments, people, and substances are draining, while others are uplifting.

At least for a while, try not to judge, but simply take notice. Then, begin to make decisions to spend less time in energy-depleting places and more time in life-giving environments and relationships.

STAY CONNECTED TO SOURCES OF INSPIRATION

Regularly ask, "Who and what inspires me?" Constant exposure to writers, poets, artists, musicians, songwriters, nature, actors, teachers, friends, and colleagues — any person or any thing that lights and fuels our inner fires — keeps us "plugged in" to supportive and sustaining sources of inspiration.

KEEP A JOURNAL

Writing or journaling, combined with daily quiet time, is an excellent tool to encourage, reflect, and "go inward." Many authentic people have developed a habit of daily journaling along with their prayer and meditation time. When combined with a clear quality of life or mission statement, journaling can be a daily report card. Journaling allows us to ask: "How did I measure up today? What events or patterns got me off track? How could I do better next time?" Journaling can be a reminder to be more mindful of being the person you are meant to be. When combined with imagery, journaling can be a useful tool to encourage positive changes.

WATCH FOR DEFINING MOMENTS

Over the years, we have met many people who are on an authentic journey. Most of them have deepened their authentic presence by facing and learning from defining moments. A defining moment can be the result of a "wake-up call," such as an illness, a death, the unplanned end of a relationship, unexpectedly losing a job, or an accident. Defining moments can also be consciously "created" — life-changing experiences as a result of the birth of a child, ending a career or a relationship, finding a mentor, or embarking on a specific adventure (running a marathon, climbing a mountain, or taking music lessons).

Regardless of whether defining moments are created or imposed, the important thing is facing them, learning from them, talking about them, and then seeing the truth in them. Unfortunately, many people experience the death of a loved one, a birth, a divorce, an illness, or even a financial windfall and continue their same patterns, never taking time to *reflect* or to *learn* from the experiences that beckon growth. If choosing a path of denial, be prepared to have the same experiences again, perhaps more intensified the next time. Life events call us to personal growth.

BE CURIOUS

Learning commences with having curiosity. According to Socrates, "Wisdom begins with wonder." Having an open, receptive, inquiring mind to everything we do brings us closer to our authentic selves. Perceiving roadblocks, failures, and conflicts as potential *learning moments* and *gifts* supports an authentic journey.

Being receptive to turning points that mean moving in a different direction is just as important as being willing to let go of old ways of thinking. A word of caution: As valuable as curiosity is to authenticity, remember to be a *student*, not a *follower*. Having openness is not necessarily the same as being in agreement. Everything we hear — including what you read in this book — must be mentally weighed and debated and matched against your own experiences and perceptions and integrated with your personal being before being called your "truth." Truths gleaned from other people, to be both useful and sustainable, must help you connect more deeply with your own truth.

CARE DAILY FOR THE SOUL

The seed of the soul within us will only take root in fertile soul. Like the environment of all life that desires to grow, one's environment must be cultivated to allow the soul to flourish.

What nourishes your soul? Create your own list or try experimenting with a few of our examples: play or listen to uplifting music; engage in art, such as painting, drawing, film, pottery, or sculpture; sing; spend time in nature; dance; read an uplifting book; connect with friends; walk on a beach; have a massage; engage in a service project; climb a mountain; go to a museum; look at the stars; play with children; watch a sunset; take a dog for a walk; spend time with elderly people; ignore a routine and try something different; buy a leather-bound journal and write in it; or just sit still. The possibilities are endless. As room is made for one's soul to express itself, identification can begin with a deeper source that is beyond the surface of our roles, our titles, and our possessions.

Now, take time to reflect upon two questions:

- "What happens to my mind, my body, and my spirit, when I neglect soul-nourishing activities for too long?"
- "What can I take out of my day today to make room for the care of my soul?"

MANAGE HUMAN HUNGERS

Have you ever been hungry when you are full? When feeling this kind of hunger, take time to ask yourself, "What am I *really* hungry for?" The human tendency to reach out for something to "fix" discomfort is illustrated by a recent ad in a London newspaper: *Harley Davidson for sale. Excellent condition. Ridden for only 6 months during a mid-life crisis.*

Feeling bad? "Buy a sports car or eat a pound cake." This is the message from an *in*authentic culture. Authenticity requires "sitting" with discomfort. Learn from it. Listen to it. Get support for it. Often discomfort is a voice from the soul. If it is smothered with booze or food or a Harley Davidson or another relationship, relief may come for a while, but the vital message of discomfort will be missed.

LEARN FROM FAILURE

An inauthentic society demands perfection, or the illusion of it, and is fearful of failure and the growth that emerges from failure. Inauthentic cultures deal with unsuccessful projects by covering up or by blaming lack of success on a convenient scapegoat.

Yet, more is learned from difficulty than from success if difficulty is faced squarely and honestly. "Every break *down* is an awaiting break *through*," David's father used to say. David's father gave this authentic response from learning to face mental illness in his own life. A most encouraging aspect of life is that a weakness can become an asset when it is faced, examined, and traced to its origin.

To climb a mountain, we need the stone crags and rough places to aid our ascent. The only way to face our weaknesses and grow is to embrace failure. Not only is embracing failure, and owning up to weaknesses that emerge, good for the soul, it is a compelling characteristic of a leader.

LET GO OF RESENTMENT

Spiritual illness results from resentment. Without having support and awareness, facing our past, acknowledging our mistakes, and beginning a process of letting go of resentments, authentic growth and an ability to impact other people will be hampered, and perhaps suffocated altogether. Letting go of resentment is not an overnight journey. It is a lifelong commitment to self-honesty. Holding on to resentment is like having toxins in the soul. Resentment is a reminder that it is not a snakebite that kills; it is the *poison*.

A myriad of symptoms can emerge which indicate resentments that need to be relinquished: rage or prolonged anger; sarcasm and demeaning, hurtful comments; unpredictable mood swings; depression; prolonged moodiness; and an inability to experience gratitude, inner peace, or kindness. Watch carefully for these symptoms. If they surface, face them. If there is a pattern, do yourself — and people you care about — a favor and get help.

BE INSPIRED BY A HIGHER PURPOSE

Having a higher purpose in life awakens new possibilities and dreams and gives sustenance in dark moments. No higher purpose is greater than being of service to other people.

Even while writing this book, we had to remind each other during the late nights and tiring days that this work was a labor of love to bring our passions and deepest desires to the world. Holding on to a vision that keeps life in perspective on the good days offers inspiration in the midst of discouragement.

STEP OUT OF CONFORMITY

We have discussed in an earlier section the task of authenticity as moving from reliance and obedience to authority and arriving at truth on the basis of personal assessment. Authenticity is about coming to trust yourself. Breaking away and following your own "bliss" will take you into the realm of great danger, but that is why it is both terrifying and appealing. There are no guides or road maps, for you are making your own map as you chart unfamiliar territory. It is like stepping into a dark forest without a path as you make your own unique trail. When you are on your own path, doors open where there were no doors before. People appear who help you along. Be receptive to the guides that come to you in all their myriad of forms, as you courageously move forward.

FOSTER COMMUNITY

The call to authentic leadership, to invest in the souls of other human beings, is also sharing the dreams and the pain of people we serve. People on an authentic journey understand that this work is far too important and far too hazardous to be done alone.

We cannot survive without meaningful connections with supportive people who can be confided in and who will make us accountable. The lone-warrior model of leadership is "valiant suicide." Each of us has blind spots and gifts that require the clarity of the vision of other people. Each of us has passions that need to be supported and contained by others. Pain, discouragement, and fear are part of an authentic journey. They require community for sustenance and healing. The Sufis had it right when they said, "The eye can't see itself." We need supportive and courageous influence from other people to see ourselves clearly.

Georgia O'Keefe, an American painter, once said, "That which is most precious to us is often so close to us that we don't know that it is there." Often an authentic person may not recognize a gift because "It feels natural — it's just who I am. It seems so ordinary that I can't imagine why anybody would want to pay that much attention to it."

Community reminds us of two things: *First*, maybe being ordinary is the source of our salvation. "Ordinariness" keeps our gift within human dimensions and protects us from having an overblown ego. *Second*, community reminds us that within the ordinariness of the gift, there is something else that is *extra*ordinary. Community honors that and supports it to come to fruition in the world. Community brings us "home" to the people with whom we belong.

There is no end to the soul's capacity to be moved in the presence of truth. Everyday, millions of people participate in 12-step programs in church basements and community halls, listening by the hour to other people sharing the truth about their lives. Listening to truth is captivating. Being in the presence of people sharing themselves inspires us to do the same. If your intentions are clear, a community will emerge.

Be open, pay attention, and be receptive. Having an authentic life as a leader depends on it.

ENDNOTES

1. As cited in Ronald A. Heifetz. 2000. *Leadership Without Easy Answers*. Cambridge, MA: Harvard University Press.

CHAPTER 6

<hr>

The Path of Authentic Leadership — Authenticity in Action

LIVING AUTHENTICALLY WITH *IN*AUTHENTICITY

In preceding chapters, we have written about recognizing authenticity, the power of living authentically, and how to become more authentic. Yet, the question remains: How can an authentic self be sustained in a culture that is inauthentic — be it a workplace, a relationship, or a community? There are no easy answers to this challenge, but we have some practical reminders for staying on track when faced with the dilemma of living authentically with inauthenticity.

Be a Lifelong Student

When up against a barrier — with a boss, a colleague, an employee, a spouse, a neighbor, or a child — remember: certain situations are to provide instruction — to teach lessons. Think about it. How else would we take the initiative to learn and grow without challenges? Treat every challenge as a potential learning opportunity, not as a barrier.

Authenticity requires curiosity. Approaching situations with a mindset for looking for possibilities instead of placing blame for being in the situation will change your demeanor. Blame leaves you impotent and helpless, but curiosity is enlightening and opens doors. Being a lifelong student also helps you remember an important quality of authentic action — having humility.

Emotional maturity is required to turn frustration into fascination. Reading books, taking classes, and gleaning enlightenment does not make you any better than anyone else. But it does indicate a thirst for growth.

Be a Source

When you are open to *being* a source of authenticity in a relationship, you become a leader, regardless of your position. Being a source means not depending on anyone or anything for authenticity.

In a culture, you are the starting place for access to authentic strength. Authentic leaders understand that real power and fulfillment come from *being* the source. When you are the source, you take full ownership for manifesting authenticity, regardless of how others respond to you. As the source, you seek to be *contributors* in a culture, rather than *consumers*. Authentic leaders have a mindset of abundance. For authentic leaders, being the source means realizing they are merely a conduit for a creative force that is available for everyone. Authentic leaders know that the supply of authentic energy is endless. From the strength of their exemplary presence, authentic leadership works tirelessly to inspire and support other people to also be the source.

Be a *Light,* Not a *Judge*

This reminder is twofold. First, "be a light." When seeking to inspire authenticity, the goal is *attraction* instead of *promotion.* The goal is having a desire for other people to *want* to join you on an authentic journey. Little good is done from coercing or manipulating other people to become more authentic. If people participate because of fear or from a need for approval, they will not stay very long because they are not being true to themselves. Participating because of fear or needing approval defeats the very purpose of an authentic journey.

No one can be forced to take a prescribed path of authenticity. Enforced behavior is inauthentic. When working with organizations, we make it clear that we are *inviting* people on a journey. It is okay to *not* come with us. No judgment is made, nor is there a "right" way to be authentic. Nothing is more repelling, nothing is more inviting for resistance, than the perception that one is being forced to be authentic. Take time to stop and ask yourself:

- "Am I a spirit of *attraction* to the people around me?"
- "Am I seen as a person who expresses the qualities of authentic action?"
- "Am I seen as having compassion, clarity, courage, and service in action?"
- "Or am I seen as having blame, bitterness, and resentment?"

If you want other people to join you, the qualities required are obvious. Remember the *Law of the Echo:* Give to the world the best that you have, and the best will come back to you — often tenfold.

Second, be "not a judge." Remember: There is no right way to be authentic. Be careful to not project a personal vision of authenticity onto other people. Authenticity attracts diversity. What is authentic for one person may not be authentic for anyone else and vice versa. For example, consider being judgmental in a marriage. Authenticity might be having verbal vulnerability — opening up and sharing — for one partner, but vulnerability and intimacy for the other person might come from actions and nonverbal expressions of love.

In relationships, respecting differences is important for personal growth and for learning from those differences. Self-righteousness is not on any list of authentic action qualities.

Let Go of Expectations

India has huge numbers of monkeys. To catch a monkey, Indians use a bottle with a neck that is just large enough for a monkey's hand to fit through it. They anchor the bottle to the ground and put a small banana in the bottle. Then they sit back and wait.

Before long, a monkey will wander by, see the banana, reach his hand into the bottle, and grab the banana. Then the monkey discovers that he cannot get his hand out of the bottle and still hold onto the banana. The monkey loudly chatters and squeals as the person who set the trap places a burlap sack over him. In the darkness of the sack, the monkey releases the banana, but by that time, he has been captured.

The monkey could let go of the banana and run away before getting caught. Some do, but most of the monkeys hang on to the banana until the sack is over their heads. Why? Because the banana has value to the monkey and the monkey is not willing to let go of that value. He is so unwilling to let go that he gives up his freedom and perhaps even his life for it. Probably everyone can identify with this story in one way or another because at one time or another, we can remember hanging on to the expectations of others as if these expectations were the basis of our survival.

Having expectations of other people is human nature. In one way or another, we are dependent on other people. The key is recognizing when dependency will suffocate us as if we were in a burlap sack. Letting go sooner is best. Remember two important principles: First, an expectation can actually be a *premeditated* resentment; and second, every time you let go, you have more power — control is gained by letting go of control.

Find a Community of Support

Living authentically in the midst of inauthenticity can be lonely and isolating. Authenticity is a lonely journey, but it cannot be undertaken alone. Regularly take an inventory of where sources of support in your life are. If you are to be a source, you need a source to draw from. When "hitting walls" and encountering resistance and continuous learning opportunities, having a community of people to draw from, people who will support you, strengthen your resolve to contribute and grow where you have been planted, and who will make you accountable to stay on track is imperative. Having a confidant who you can open up to makes letting go and maintaining perspective much easier.

Seek support from a caring community. Everyone needs people for support, even if they are not the people you care most about, because being authentic can hurt. When people do not "come along" with us, it can be painful. On some days, being authentic is wearying, and even exhausting.

Stay the Course

Inevitably, if remaining committed to authentic development, this question will arise: "When is it time to leave an inauthentic environment or relationship?" To answer this question, be clear: exiting must always be an option — but as a *last* resort. Knowing where the fire exits are and how to find them if you need them is important. But do not dwell on the exit. Dwell on the work that lies before you.

Before contemplating leaving a relationship, ensure that the lessons to be learned from being in the relationship have been learned. Sometimes the lessons to be learned are not clear. We have found that it is generally wise to stay put until you have wrestled long enough to gain a reasonable degree of clarity. We know that leaving a relationship too early — at work, in a career, in a business partnership, in a marriage, or in a friendship — will simply set you up against the same barrier in the next relationship. Barriers are to *learn* from, not to *run* from.

Remember the Serenity Prayer

The *Serenity Prayer* was written many years ago by Reinhold Niebuhr (1892–1971). An excerpt from this prayer is a source of strength and guidance for bringing your authentic self into the workplace and into life. In the words of Niebuhr: "God, give me the serenity to accept the things I cannot change, the courage to change the things I can, and the wisdom to know the difference." For us, three rules have emerged from this simple prayer:

- *Change the changeable.* Focus on things that are within your control, within your circle of influence, namely your responses to the world.

- *Accept the unchangeable.* Let go of your need to change anyone or anything. This is not because doing so will put you on some kind of moral higher ground, but because it just will not work. (Anyone who has been in a relationship longer than 2 days knows the truth in this.)

- *Remove yourself from the unacceptable.* If being authentic in your current situation puts your core values or your safety at risk, to remain authentic you must remove yourself from that situation — either psychologically or geographically.

Track Progress

Connecting with yourself and your environment enables you to be attuned to things following you and things you are following. Work with indigenous peoples has taught us about devices to track our progress toward our higher purpose.[1] Tracking your stress levels, because stress is an indicator that something has gone awry, is a way to track your environment and yourself within an environment. Stop, look, and listen to stress.

Follow stress to its source. Is it authentic, or healthy, stress — the stress of being authentic in an inauthentic environment — or inauthentic, destructive stress — the stress of living *removed* from your authentic self? Is it stress by choice? We encourage you to *choose* the kind of stress that you experience. Being a victim and blaming an inauthentic system will only reinforce your capacity to remain inauthentic and experience destructive stress. Instead, think about where the deep satisfaction of being authentic and living in accord with your deepest values can be experienced.

Another way of tracking your current environment and yourself within that environment is to examine your level of life-giving energy. Indigenous peoples say that we are still "alive" (and thus receptive to authenticity) if we can track the four "rivers" of life:

Inspiration. If you are still alive, you can be inspired and uplifted. *Finding Neverland*, a beautiful movie, illustrates how inspiration can emerge from children. Who and what things are sources of inspiration for you?

Challenge. If you are still alive, you can be challenged and tested. Being open to challenge invites personal growth, moving beyond the knowable, and stretching. Who or what things are stretching and challenging you?

Surprise. If you are still alive, you can be delighted by surprises and the unexpected. This is a characteristic of childhood. Children are open to awe and curiosity as a natural part of life. Cynicism dries up our "river" of surprise. Remain alive by having a connection with wonder and awe and curiosity. Each day is filled with surprises that can often be found in between scheduled events. Be open to surprise.

Love. Love comes from being deeply touched and moved by life. Are your hearts *open*? A friend of ours said quadruple open-heart bypass surgery was required to "open" his heart to living. Being alive and receptive to being authentic is being open and having four other heart chambers: a full heart, an open heart, a clear heart, and a strong heart.

Take time to ask yourself: Where am I half-hearted rather than full-hearted? Where do I have a closed-heart rather than an open-heart? Where am I weak-hearted rather than strong-hearted?

There is no vaccine or immunity to love. Nothing keeps us from loving. Thinking that we must close our hearts in order to set boundaries is having a spiritual illusion. Being weak-hearted is lacking the courage to be who we are. On the other hand, being strong-hearted is finding the courage to bring our authentic selves to life. Strong-hearted people know they make a difference.

We believe that more strong-hearted authentic leaders are desperately needed in the world.

AUTHENTIC COMMUNITIES

In and through community lies the salvation of the world.
—M. Scott Peck

Sometimes we talk about all sorts of things with a person who is sitting next to us on an airplane, someone we will never see again, but then we come home and withdraw or isolate ourselves from a life partner of many years. Many people are lonely and closed off because they have no meaningful connections, no one who affirms and supports them.

What Is a Community?

In a society of enduring individualism, where there is apprehension about being vulnerable or honest about ourselves, community can have a myriad of meanings. Today, the word community can be defined as almost any assortment of people — a town, a neighborhood, a professional association, a church, or a synagogue — regardless of the quality of the relationships within that group. Community is from the root word *com*, meaning *together* or *with*, combined with *union*, meaning *coming together with others* and *finding union*.

What Is an Authentic Community?

Our definition of community is somewhat different. Our definition is finding *union* with at least one person with whom we can communicate honestly and with whom our relationship is more substantive than only maintaining a pretense of composure. To find meaning in the word community, our definition must at least connote a group of people that honors our authentic selves and is committed to having a reciprocal relationship that supports, encourages, and makes us accountable for being ourselves and the best people we can be.

Continuing to support a society that is concerned only with individual rights, that pursues comfort more than self-honesty, and that values accumulation more than connection means living in a world that is fragmented, closed in, and incapable of promoting authenticity — and we ultimately end up lonely. But how do we find an authentic community?

Create an Authentic Community

Better than finding an authentic community is *creating* one. In striving to create an authentic community, what would one be like? How would it function? A first step would be to reflect on several questions:

- What does real community mean to me?
- Who supports my authentic journey to be all I can be?
- Who helps me look at myself more deeply — beyond the self I typically present to the world?
- Who can I be honest with about myself?
- Who makes me accountable for staying on track, for living in accord with my values and a higher purpose?
- Where do I go where I know I am loved?
- Where am I permitted, encouraged, and supported to be authentic?

As you take time to reflect upon and answer these questions, some of you will realize that you already have elements of community in your life. If so, express appreciation and gratitude to everyone who supports and encourages you to be authentic. On the other hand, some of you will notice incongruity or discrepancy between your current relationships and the relationships that you want to have. Yearning for relationships that are beyond the superficial and looking for communities that are more real and honest encourages authenticity.

Once again, remember: An authentic journey requires you to surround yourself with authentic people. Authentic people are attracted to communities where they can support and encourage authenticity in other people. They want to be with like-hearted authentic people and have a commitment to nurture this desire in other people. Giving yourself permission to be authentic often begins with finding others that will give you this permission.

Our Vision of an Authentic Community
It Is Not the Community Your Grandparents Had

Sometimes we long for the "good old days." Some people even wish for the days when pioneer neighbors experienced community barn raising and quilting bees. Those days certainly had elements of a strong sense of community that may still be found in some of our communities, but, for the most part, these elements are missing in many modern-day neighborhoods. Yet they did not necessarily have the fruits of the authentic community that we are proposing.

When asked about his relationship to his wife, David's grandfather said: "I worked three jobs to keep food on the table during the depression years, while your grandmother raised the children and helped the neighbors. We didn't have time for much of this 'closeness' that is talked about today."

His sustaining love for his wife was evident, but so was the pain of being alone, which he experienced throughout a life of hard work and rugged individualism and from knowing he had few tools to express his authentic desires.

Instead, It Is a Vision

Our vision proposes returning to a community, but not to the same community that our grandparents had. Our vision of an authentic community is one in which a community is supportive and encouraging. It is a safe place to:

- Learn to accept who I am, along with my strengths and weaknesses, and be honored for the unique contributions I make with my distinct gifts.

- Learn to accept and love others for who they are, not for what I think they should be.

- Experience ongoing learning and development in all areas of my life.

- Fill my soul with a sense of belonging, so that my authentic journey is supported.

- Be supported to explore and discover a higher purpose for my life.

- Be around people who see beyond my possessions and roles to who I am inside.

- Honor diversity and inclusion among members. Among the highest attributes of an authentic community is its capacity to respect a multiplicity of expressions of the human experience. Bev Suek said, "I'm a big supporter of diversity. I like to surround myself with people who are different than I am. It is so energizing to have people who disagree with me."

- Work for a greater purpose beyond the community itself.

- Be held accountable. People in an authentic community should not only support me, but also *challenge* me to evolve to become my best. In an authentic community, I can speak openly of my deepest aspirations and feel reciprocal support for upholding my commitments.

- Develop all my qualities of authentic presence.

- Move, but not expecting to do so perfectly, toward a vision of authentic growth, both within and between members. Authentic communities are similar to authentic people. Rather than trying to portray an illusion of perfection, they are dedicated to seeking, discerning, and moving toward truth. People within an authentic community speak openly about how a community supports or hinders their personal journey.

When making a personal list of requirements of an authentic community, our vision, as listed above, might seem lofty and idealistic. Yet, many people are willing to embrace a vision such as this and move in the direction of having an authentic community. Our list is a reminder. It is our vision for finding a little more authenticity in our relationships.

People who are not in an authentic community that exhibits the qualities on our list, but who have an understanding of what an authentic community is, will allow themselves to ask questions and make conscious choices about what they do with their time and who they spend their time with: "Is this a place where I will be accepted for who I am? Is this a place that will encourage me and challenge me to grow and be my best? Or is this not that place?"

SPONTANEOUS AUTHENTIC LEADERSHIP
IN A CRISIS

Authentic Leadership Is Different

It is the responsibility of transformational, authentic leadership to shift from *assigning* blame to *assuming* personal accountability. Authentic leadership is making a commitment to have a positive impact, which inevitably comes to fruition when we shift from saying "I can't make a difference," to asking "*How* can I make a difference?" So much of the work of authentic leadership is inspiring ourselves and others to find the courage to take the higher ground of personal accountability.

In Biloxi

In fall of 2005, in the long, harrowing hours before Hurricane Katrina crashed into Biloxi, Mississippi, 14 family members, friends, and neighbors piled into the only bedroom of a wooden house and waited... until the water rushed in. Then babies began to scream, children began to cry, and the adults panicked, but 13-year-old Phillip Bullard began to save lives.[2]

Phillip swam, cradling the youngest children. He floated the oldest people through the house, out of a broken front window, and into a boat that was floating down the street. He coaxed his twin sister to hold onto the side of the house, which she did in sheer terror. Then he went underwater to clear a path to a window where he could rescue his oldest sister. He rescued her first because she was the only other person who could swim and help him get the rest of the people out of the house to safety.

Next, Phillip took his mother and grandmother, who were unable to swim and too frightened to leave the house, by the hand and led them through the house on top of sodden furniture. When Phillip finally swam out of the house, he found his twin sister still clinging to the exterior wall. Later, Phillip said quietly, "She was scared. It took me a while to convince her to let go and take my hand. But I had to keep on trying because she wouldn't have made it."

After everyone was rescued, Phillip took the boat to a main thoroughfare to find help, but it never came. So he organized the family and their friends and used broomsticks to paddle down the street to a house where they could take haven in a neighbor's upstairs loft.

Phillip is a soft-spoken seventh-grade student. He eventually ended up in a shelter at the school that he normally attends. He was called a hero in this small town because he saved the lives of four adults and nine children. Phillip does not see himself as a hero. "I was just scared that if I didn't keep helping, somebody would die."

The story of Phillip Bullard is one of hundreds that emerged from the Hurricane Katrina catastrophe. It illustrates authentic leadership that is spontaneous in times of crisis.

In New Orleans

Many other stories were told about heroism from within the ranks of ordinary citizens in New Orleans. Maintenance workers used fork lifts to carry the sick and disabled; engineers rigged generators and kept them running; nurses took over mechanical ventilators and spent hours on end manually forcing air into the lungs of unconscious patients to keep them alive; mechanics helped hot-wire any car that could be found to ferry people out of the city; and food service workers scoured commercial kitchens improvising meals for hundreds of stranded people. Most of these workers had lost their homes and had not heard from their families, yet they stayed and provided the only infrastructure possible for the 20% of New Orleans that was not under water.[3]

These are examples of spontaneous, authentic leadership at its finest, yet on the other side of the page, numerous stories told accounts of thugs who used the disaster in New Orleans as an excuse for an orgy of pillaging, armed robbery, and rape. The buses that arrived to evacuate people were stormed. Police officers became criminals. Doctors trying to treat patients at the Superdome were attacked. Looters brazenly ransacked stores, businesses, and homes, looking for food, alcohol, clothing, electronics, appliances, and guns.

Some years ago, a journalist and philosopher wrote about all of us being only 48 hours from complete anarchy if the structure of our society were displaced. In 2005, New Orleans certainly seemed to prove this point. Perhaps below the surface of these stories about New Orleans is the real nature of who we are as a society and what our authentic nature really is — both magnificent and evil. The disaster witnessed in New Orleans did not happen over a period of days. It had been happening for decades. Hurricane Katrina merely exposed it to public view, just as any crisis will expose us to ourselves.

It has been said that circumstances do not *determine* a person; rather, they *reveal* a person. Tragedies that bring us to death's door invite *realness*, to be "who we are" as people. Catastrophes strip away the masks and façades that we use to surround ourselves, revealing our authentic core. Reflect on crises you, people you know, or people you lead have faced. Then ask: "What kind of leadership emerges from *me* in times of crisis?"

Momentous catastrophes such as New Orleans and Hurricane Katrina, New York in September 2001, or the London subway attacks in the summer of 2005 may some day personally affect us. More likely, we will be confronted by a far less severe tragedy, yet every bit as significant, such as death, a life-threatening illness, loss of a job, an accident, bankruptcy, or a natural disaster. What kind of a leader will emerge from our authentic presence in moments of crisis and need? What person is within us? What person will come forward when disaster strikes?

In times of crisis when appropriate leadership is lacking, the road most traveled is the road of blame, resentment, and gossip. It is always easier to point our fingers at other people for not doing what we are unwilling or incapable of doing. It is easy to use self-righteous opinions and bitterness as a shield against acknowledging our sense of helplessness, fear, and grief. It is much harder to shift conversation from blaming to having personal accountability.

In Canada

Terry Fox was an authentic individual whose answer to "How can I make a difference?" transformed and united an entire country — and beyond. Raised in Port Coquitlam, British Columbia, Terry was an active teenager who participated in many sports. In 1977, when he was only 18 years old, Terry was diagnosed with Osteogenic Sarcoma (bone cancer). His right leg was amputated 6 inches above the knee. While in the hospital, Terry was so overcome by the plight of other cancer patients (many were young children) that he decided to run across Canada to raise money for cancer research. Terry said: "Somewhere the hurting must stop." He called his journey the *Marathon of Hope*.

After 18 months and running over 5000 kilometers in preparation for the run, Terry started his run in St. John's, Newfoundland on April 12, 1980 with little fanfare. Although it was difficult to garner attention in the beginning, enthusiasm soon grew, and the money collected along his route began to grow. He ran 42 kilometers a day through Canada's Atlantic Provinces, Quebec, and Ontario. It was a journey that Canadians will never forget.

On September 1, 1981, after 143 days and 5373 kilometers, outside of Thunder Bay, Ontario, Terry was forced to stop running before he collapsed from exhaustion. Cancer had reappeared in his lungs. An entire nation was stunned and saddened.

This heroic Canadian was forced to stop running, but his legacy was just beginning. On February 1, 1981, only 5 months before his death on June 28, Terry's "unimaginable dream" of raising $1 from every Canadian to fight cancer was realized. The population of Canada at that time was 24.1 million people. Terry Fox's *Marathon of Hope* fund totaled $24.17 million. To date, more than

$400 million has been raised in over 400 countries for cancer research in Terry's name through the annual Terry Fox Run.[4]

If Terry were alive today, in all likelihood, he would not tell us that he set out on a mission to be an "authentic leader." Instead, he would probably say that he had a vision to use the talents he had been given to serve others. A spontaneous act of generosity, of passionately pursuing our highest aspirations beyond our self-interest, is the heart of true authentic leadership. It is not the power of our position, but the strength of our presence that attracts other people.

Authentic Leadership Is Being Accountable

St. Francis of Assisi (1181–1226), patron saint of animals and ecology, in a prayer written hundreds of years ago, speaks of authentic, transformational leadership from assuming personal accountability.[5] As St. Francis faced his own painful experiences of ill health and ridicule, this prayer expressed his desire in response to personal crisis:

A Simple Prayer

Lord, make me an instrument of your peace.

Where there is hatred, let me sow love.

Where there is injury, pardon.

Where there is discord, unity.

Where there is doubt, faith.

Where there is error, truth.

Where there is despair, hope.

Where there is sadness, joy.

Where there is darkness, light.

O, Divine Master, grant that I may not so much seek

To be consoled as to console.

To be understood as to understand.

To be loved as to love.

For

It is in giving that we receive.

It is in pardoning that we are pardoned.

And it is in dying that we are born to eternal life.

To paraphrase,

... For it is by self-forgetting that one finds.

It is by forgiving that one is forgiven.

It is by dying that one awakens to Eternal Life. Amen.

May St. Francis of Assisi, Phillip Bullard, Terry Fox, and all of the men and women we meet in life, whose responses from authentic leadership emerge spontaneously in times of need, be a source of strength and inspiration to all people[6] who are committed to following the path of authenticity.

ENDNOTES

1. Angeles Arrien. 1994. *Gathering Medicine: Stories, Songs and Methods for Soul-Retrieval: Traveling the Four-Fold Path to Find Your Personal Truth* (audio cassette: exploration of soul retrieval among indigenous peoples). Boulder, CO: Sounds True.

2. Audra Burch. "Teen Rescues Family from Certain Death." *Calgary Herald*, September 1, 2005.

3. Larry Bradshaw and Lorrie Beth Slonsky. *Hurricane Katrina —
Our Experiences*. EMS Network. Available at:
http://www.emsnetwork.org/artman/publish/article_18427
.shtml.

4. For information about The Terry Fox Foundation and the annual Terry Fox Run, contact: www.terryfoxrun.org.

5. A prayer attributed to St. Francis of Assisi (1181–1226) from the
1982 *Book of Common Prayer*.

6. Many thanks and deep appreciation for the wisdom and insights
of Warren Harbeck, a friend and coffee companion, who
inspired this chapter. Conversations with Warren, and the
perspectives that emerged from our dialogues, have made
me a better person.

Concluding Reflections
— A Call to Action

Recently, we had a conversation with "Brad," a 40-year-old, typical type A personality who had aggressively embarked on an authentic journey. He said, "I really must find my purpose. I'm passionate about it. I don't know what it is, but I'm feeling really good about myself, and I need to find my purpose. I've got to find it."

We quickly said, "Hey, take a time out. We hear you saying that your purpose in life is to do something really big, something 'out there,' like saving Africa, stopping hunger, or curing AIDS."

After a few moments of reflection, we prefaced a question with: "We're here to learn from every person we meet and to teach in every situation we find ourselves in. What if your purpose were simply to just be Brad? Are you willing to put that on your list of possible purposes in life? Are you willing to simply stay with the struggle, be open to learning about yourself, and then share that with others?"

After taking a break for a couple of hours and some reflection, he said, "I think I've got it. I think I know what my purpose is. I don't have to go out and make a quest for it anymore. This feels really good. I can just be Brad, constantly learning more about myself and helping others in this same process."

BEING AUTHENTIC WILL BRING CONTENTMENT

Welcome to the world of authentic leadership. If you have made a simple and courageous decision to be more of yourself and bring your authentic self to everything you do, you are "doing it." It is not necessary to go out there and stress yourself out. Relax, and it will come to you.

We know that for some people (ourselves included), it does not seem to be that simple! We often say, "It's got to be more than that!" But it really is not. Find out more about yourself and share it when you have an opportunity. Reach out and support someone who is struggling. Allow them to invite you in, or not, without judgment. Everyone moves at a different pace.

Try not to get too frustrated with yourself when everything does not "all come together." We do not have crystal clear clarity either, but we think constantly listening to an inner calling, listening to the voice inside us, searching for and trying to integrate the things that make sense, and discarding the things that do not fit is a worthwhile struggle. We have had many "alone" times and probably will continue to have them. For now, we have some clarity, but we suspect that when we are ready for new growth, lack of clarity will return. This just seems to be the way life is. It is a cycle. It is not waking up with a monumental "aha" moment and that is the end of it.

Remember what Jock McKeen says: "… All of the self-awareness that I've had over the years could be thrown away in a minute if I started to believe that this is really true rather than that I'm a work in progress."

Authenticity is an ongoing, recurring learning process. Never ever give up on it. Dark periods will pass just as enlightened moments do. So far we have never run into a "double night" or a "double day" (of course, unless one resides above the Arctic Circle). We have sleepless nights of agony and isolation, just as we have moments of ecstasy and jubilation. It is all part of the journey. Listen to yourself. Trust yourself. This is a pilgrim's journey. There is no prescription or easy road to take to open up and become your full self.

IF THERE IS NO QUICK FIX, THEN WHAT?

We cannot offer a prescription, a quick fix, easy answers, or a road map. Instead, you can *allow yourself* the permission to acknowledge that the callings, inner voices, and yearnings for something beyond the things that the world presently offers are valid and should be acknowledged. A price will be paid for attention given to callings and yearnings, just as an even bigger price is paid for ignoring them. We believe that many illnesses of the modern-day world are from the stress of not listening to or acknowledging inner callings. Yet, we are continually amazed that lessons appear when we are ready and open for them.

FINAL THOUGHTS ABOUT THIS BOOK

Writing this book has been an amazing journey. Besides the synergy that developed from our growing friendship as we began to write over a year ago, this book has had a life-changing role in our careers and in our lives. Working on this project together has been a fabulous experience of personal development.

Our lives have been enriched by the connections with authentic leaders who graciously gave of their time, by the powerful conversations, and by the opportunities for self-reflection that came from working together. Writing this book has given us a renewed focus by taking us on a journey that looked at our lives, our insights, and the people and events that led us to where we are today. We have examined carefully our current beliefs and how we are manifesting them today.

Writing this book has also helped crystallize our individual and collective purpose. We have a sense of clarity about our higher purpose, which is to inspire and guide leaders who are committed to making a difference to authentically connect with themselves and with the people they serve so that they may amplify their personal impact and, in the process, find deeper meaning and contentment in their lives.

We are excited about the possibilities of this book for the reader. Read it. Evaluate it. Value or discard it. Take what fits and leave the rest. We are better people for having struggled to articulate and live according to the principles we have written about. May the same be true for you.

Timpanogos Cave — The Power and Challenge of Vision

Tell me, what is it you plan to do with your one wild and precious life?
—Mary Oliver, The Summer Day

In August 1921, a cave was rediscovered, high on the wall of a small canyon in northern Utah. Later that year, the subsequent discovery of another cave in the same area renewed a great interest in caves and caving.

Local citizens approached the U.S. Forest Service, which had responsibility for the land where the caves were located, asking when tours of the caves would begin. The Forest Service responded that there was no extra money and therefore there would be no tours, but agreed to place a gate on the entrance and secure it with a lock.

One group of local citizens was not pleased with this answer and took it upon themselves to form the Timpanogos Cave Committee and return to the Forest Service with a plan of their own. The Committee would raise the money required, build a trail up the

211

canyon wall, install lights in the cave, and conduct tours. The Forest Service did not have to do anything but say "yes." The Forest Service agreed to the plan, with one condition: if the Committee ever made a profit, the extra money would be reinvested in making further improvements to the area.

With an agreement in place, the Committee spent the winter of 1921–1922 building a mile-long trail up the canyon wall to reach the cave entrance that was 1200 feet above the canyon floor. While the trail to the cave was being built, electrical wires were run to the cave entrance and lights and wiring were installed inside the cave. The committee opened the cave to the public in 1922.

In 1922, the Timpanogos Cave was declared a National Monument. During the ensuing 25 years, even while responsibility for the cave was being transferred to the National Park Service, the Committee continued operations. The Committee remained true to their word and reinvested profits into improving the area. Tunnels were blasted to provide access to two other caves. The trail was rerouted and rebuilt to provide access to newly opened areas. Restrooms and other visitor facilities were constructed.

More than 80 years later, the legacy of the dedication of this small group of Committee members still remains because they fell in love with an idea and made it happen.

The brief history of this magnificent National Monument was told by a guide, Royce Shelley, in the summer of 2004. Royce is a schoolteacher. He spends his summers conducting tours through the caves. His passion and love of the caves is contagious. Around every bend in the cave is a new adventure. Royce tells story after story about the history of stalagmites and stalactites and the magic that can be found in each of these special formations. His soul is alive in these caves. His love for his work touches people daily, perhaps more than the beauty of the caves themselves.

At the end of a tour, while visitors' eyes adjust from the darkness of the cave to the sunlight, Royce shares his passion and love for these magnificent caves:

> Here is a challenge for you, and it isn't to find your own cave. Most of us will never discover a cave, but each of us has an opportunity to discover something that we truly care about, something that we love. It might be music, mathematics, art, dance, languages, science, athletics, neighborhood parks, or a million other things. The challenge is to use our lives and talents so that 100 years from now, life will be better for people and for this planet because we were here, just like our lives are better today because of the Timpanogos Cave Committee.

In some ways, authentic leadership is similar to the story about the Timpanogos Cave Committee. Authentic leadership expresses passion, caring, and a deep commitment to a purpose beyond self-interest. It is the deepest expression of the human spirit in leadership that awakens, inspires, and guides people to be all they can be.

In this one wild and precious life, each of us leaves a legacy. What will be yours?

Bibliography

Autry, J. 2001. *The Servant Leader: How to Build a Creative Team, Develop Great Morale, and Improve Bottom-Line Performance.* New York: Three Rivers Press.

_____. 1991. *Love and Profit: The Art of Caring Leadership.* New York: Avon Books.

Bellman, G. 2002. *The Consultant's Calling: Bringing Who You Are to What You Do.* San Francisco: Jossey-Bass.

_____. 1996. *Your Signature Path: Gaining New Perspectives on Life and Work.* San Francisco: Berrett-Koehler.

Block, P. 1996. *Stewardship: Choosing Service over Self-Interest.* San Francisco: Berrett-Koehler.

_____. 2000. *The Answer to How Is Yes: Acting on What Matters.* San Francisco: Berrett-Koehler.

Collins, J. 2001. *Good to Great: Why Some Companies Make the Leap... and Others Don't.* New York: HarperBusiness.

Gerber, R. 2002. *Leadership the Eleanor Roosevelt Way: Timeless Strategies from the First Lady of Courage.* New York: Prentice Hall.

Gibb, J.R. 1978. *Trust: A New View of Personal and Organizational Development.* Los Angeles: Guild of Tutors Press.

Heifetz, R. 2000. *Leadership Without Easy Answers.* Cambridge, MA: Harvard University Press.

Hendricks, G. and K. Ludeman. 1996. *The Corporate Mystic: A Guidebook for Visionaries with Their Feet on the Ground.* New York: Bantam Books.

Hiebert, M. and B. Klatt. 2001. *The Encyclopedia of Leadership: A Practical Guide to Popular Leadership Theories and Techniques.* New York: McGraw-Hill.

Hillman, J. 1996. *The Soul's Code: In Search of Character and Calling.* New York: Random House.

Irvine, D., B. Klatt, and S. Murphy. 2003. *Accountability: Getting a Grip on Results.* Calgary, Alberta, Canada: Bow River Publishing.

Irvine, D. 2003. *Becoming Real: Journey to Authenticity.* Sanford, FL: DC Press.

_____. 2004. *Simple Living in a Complex World: A Guide to Balancing Life's Achievements.* Toronto, Ontario, Canada: Wiley & Sons Canada.

Izzo, J. 2004. *Second Innocence: Rediscovering Joy and Wonder: A Guide to Renewal in Work, Relationships, and Daily Life.* San Francisco: Berrett-Koehler.

Lowney, C. 2003. *Heroic Leadership: Best Practices from a 450-Year-Old Company that Changed the World.* Chicago: Loyola Press.

Marrella, L. 2005. *In Search of Ethics: Conversations with Men and Women of Character.* Sanford, FL: DC Press.

Savory, A. 1999. *Holistic Management.* Washington, DC: Island Press.

Spears, L. and M. Lawrence, Eds. 2002. *Focus on Leadership: Servant-Leadership for the 21st Century.* New York: Wiley & Sons.

Weinberg, G. 2002. *More Secrets of Consulting: The Consultant's Tool Kit.* New York: Dorset House Publishing.

Whyte, D. 2001. *Crossing the Unknown Sea: Work as a Pilgrimage of Identity.* New York: Riverhead Books.

Wong, B. and J. McKeen. 1998. *The [New] Manual for Life.* Gabriola Island, British Columbia, Canada: PD Publishing; www.haven.ca

For Additional Informaton

If this book has inspired you or if you would like to receive information on our presentations, programs, or coaching, we invite you to contact us:

David Irvine
The Leader's Navigator
Box 358
Cochrane, Alberta,
Canada
T4C 1A6
Email: david@davidirvine.com
Website: www.davidirvine.com

Jim Reger
The Reger Group
110 — 2659 Douglas Street
Victoria, British Columbia,
Canada
V8T 4M3
Email: jim@regergroup.com
Website: www.regergroup.com

If you found this book thought provoking…
If you are interested in having this author
or another of our consulting authors
design a workshop or seminar for your
company, organization, school, or team…

Let the experienced and knowledgeable group of experts
at *The Diogenes Consortium* go to work for you.
With literally hundreds of years of combined experience in:

Ethics • Human Resources • Employee Retention
Management • Pro-Active Leadership • Teams
Encouragement • Empowerment • Motivation
Attitute Modification • Energizing • Delegating Responsibility
Spirituality in the Workplace
Presentations to start-ups and Fortune 500 companies,
tax-exempt organizations and schools of all sizes
(public & private, elementary through university)

Call today for a list of our
authors/speakers/presenters/consultants
Call toll free at 866-602-1476
Or visit:
www.FocusOnEthics.com